5/23

What It Is

Also by Clifford Thompson

Twin of Blackness: A Memoir
Love for Sale and Other Essays
Signifying Nothing: A Novel

Clifford Thompson

WHAT IT IS

Race, Family, and
One Thinking Black Man's Blues

Other Press
New York

Baldwin epigraph from *Nobody Knows My Name* © 1961 by James Baldwin.
Copyright renewed. Published by Vintage Books. Used by arrangement with
the James Baldwin Estate. Descartes epigraph reprinted courtesy of Early
Modern Texts (www.earlymoderntexts.com). Translation compiled from
multiple sources by Jonathan Bennett, copyright © Jonathan Bennet 2017.

Interior illustrations by Clifford Thompson.

Production editor: Yvonne E. Cárdenas
Text designer: Julie Fry
This book was set in Legacy and Dispatch.

10 9 8 7 6 5 4 3 2

Library of Congress Cataloging-in-Publication Data
Names: Thompson, Clifford, author.
Title: What it is : race, family, and one thinking Black man's blues /
    Clifford Thompson.
Description: New York : Other Press, [2019]
Identifiers: LCCN 2019007819 (print) | LCCN 2019980921 (ebook) |
    ISBN 9781590519059 (hardcover) | ISBN 9781590519066 (ebook)
Subjects: LCSH: Thompson, Clifford. | Thompson, Clifford—Political and
    social views. | Trump, Donald, 1946- —Public opinion. | African American
    authors—Biography. | African Americans—Social conditions—1975- |
    African Americans—Race identity. | Whites—United States—Attitudes. |
    United States—Race relations. | United States—Social conditions—
    21st century.
Classification: LCC PS3570.H59683 Z46 2019 (print) | LCC PS3570.H59683 (ebook) |
    DDC 814/.54 [B]—dc23
LC record available at https://lccn.loc.gov/2019007819
LC ebook record available at https://lccn.loc.gov/2019980921

For my daughters

But I still believe that the unexamined life is not worth living: and I know that self-delusion, in the service of no matter what small or lofty cause, is a price no writer can afford. His subject is himself and the world and it requires every ounce of stamina he can summon to attempt to look on himself and the world as they are.

— James Baldwin, *Nobody Knows My Name*

The seeker after truth must once in his lifetime doubt everything that he can doubt.

—René Descartes, *Principles of Philosophy*

Introduction

I am a black man, Brooklyn-based, fifty-four years old as I write this. For nearly as long as I can remember, there has been, at the core of my being, making me who I am, or who I feel that I am, the belief that I must treat everyone as an individual, that I must not base my judgments on anything as inconsequential as skin color. And for most of my adult life, I have chosen to see myself as an American, because of the contributions black people have made to this country, because of how inextricably this country is tied to my heritage, and despite white racists' belief that the country is theirs more than it is mine.

Living according to these principles has sometimes been tough. In my late teens and twenties, moving from the all-black environment where I grew up to integrated circles in college and beyond, I sometimes felt like the only black person I knew who was not reluctant—

because of distrust, dislike, or both—to be in the predominantly white settings where my interests often took me. I clung stubbornly to my beliefs, and in my mid-twenties I found what I considered to be support for my point of view when I picked up, somewhat belatedly, the books of James Baldwin. Leaving aside, for a moment, the music of Baldwin's sentences, the grandness of his vision, the wisdom and lyricism he brings to expressing the anger and ache of being black in America, he was the first model I found of one who brought everything he had to bear on opposing racism *without being racist himself.* His fiction, particularly the underappreciated *Tell Me How Long the Train's Been Gone*, and his nonfiction, none more eloquent than *The Fire Next Time*, are the work of a man who rages at injustice but loves deeply and without regard to pigmentation. While the assassinations of Medgar Evers, Malcolm X, and Martin Luther King Jr., along with other aspects of the backlash against the civil rights movement, left Baldwin embittered and disillusioned, they did not ultimately compromise his humanity or make him into a racist. He remained, for me, a model of how to conduct oneself with regard to race.

And yet I still felt some confusion. There was one substantive difference between me and the white people in my circle: being white, I discovered, seemed to make one exempt from the question of who one is. They were Americans, these white people, and it never seemed to occur to them, and certainly no one ever indicated to them, that they should think otherwise. Many black people, of course, are exempt from this question of who they are, too, by virtue of living and working largely or wholly among other blacks. But if a person's life and interests take him — as mine have taken me — to places where he looks different from most others, that person may begin to ask where the similarities between himself and these others end and the differences, beyond the obvious one, begin; what the basis for these similarities is, and what the basis for the differences is; and into which camp — similarity or difference? — nationality falls.

And with regard to the very question of whether nationality constitutes a bond or barrier between oneself and others — the basis of *this* question is an unspoken assumption that runs so deep, that is reinforced so often and in so many ways, that I passed three decades of life on Earth before I questioned it. The assumption? That *being American means being white*. At best, the place of blacks in all this seemed to be the one described by the comedian Chris Rock, who said that for us, America is like the uncle who molested you and then paid for your college education.

As much as I would like to say that I began to question that assumption on my own, I had help. It was the work of the essayist Stanley Crouch, which in turn led me to the work of his mentor (and soon to be mine), Albert Murray, that opened my eyes. Murray's books, beginning with *The Omni-Americans*, proposed an alternate view: that America, rather than being simply a white monster that feeds on people of color and that only the most self-hating of dark-skinned folks would identify with, is in fact largely a black creation—in terms of everything from culture to physical labor—and that the blood, sweat, and investment of generations of blacks makes America our home as much as it is anyone's. According to this view, the struggles blacks have historically faced have provided the obstacles over which we demonstrated the ability to triumph. As Murray wrote in *The Omni-Americans*: "The legendary exploits of white U.S. backwoodsmen, keelboatmen, and prairie schoonermen…become relatively *safe* when one sets them beside the breathtaking escapes of the fugitive slave beating his way south to Florida, west to the Indians, and north to far away Canada through swamp and town alike seeking *freedom*—nobody was chasing Daniel Boone!" To say "I am an American," then, is not an act of capitulation but the first step toward claiming one's birthright, recognizing the setting of one's ancestors' triumphs and adventures; it is tantamount to saying, "I am home."

The symbol for this idea, the art form that allows me to celebrate this notion of laying claim to a home, birthright, and identity, is jazz. The basis of jazz, a black contribution to American and world culture, is improvisation—a metaphor for the story of black Americans, who have historically had to make a way where none existed before, a way that brought about both the Underground Railroad and the civil rights movement. Every time a jazz musician improvises a passage, he or she celebrates this history. I embraced the sound and what it stood for: the fleet-footed sweetness of the alto saxophonist Julian "Cannonball" Adderley, the crusty vulnerability of Ben Webster's tenor sax, the spare melancholy of Miles Davis's trumpet, the sheer might of the original tenor man, Coleman Hawkins, the beautiful eccentricity of Thelonious Monk's piano, the deceptive laziness of Billie Holiday's voice, the doggedness and inventiveness of the young Freddie Hubbard as he played trumpet lines over and through the thundering drumbeats of Art Blakey — the doggedness and inventiveness necessary for survival, for any jazz musician, any black person, anyone at all.

And so, in my early thirties, a youngish man and new father to a biracial child, a budding essayist who earned his living as an editor and copyeditor, a seeker after cultural knowledge, with Murray in my head and Baldwin in my heart, I set out into the big bad world: reading book after book while straphanging on my way to and from work, listening at night to those jazz records that were the record of my people's contribution, believing all the while in the rightness of calling myself an American, as years, and then two decades, passed. Along the way, the first black president was elected, which appeared to confirm what I had already decided. Along the way, events may have chipped at the outside of my beliefs; killings of blacks, from Trayvon Martin on through Eric Garner, Sandra Bland, Tamir Rice, and so many others, may have led me to question whether I really wanted to call home a place where the police were seemingly paid to kill people who looked like me. And yet neither Baldwin nor Murray had ever said that I wouldn't have to fight to protect my place in this land I called home. With many others, I took to the streets over those killings and believed I was doing so in service of my country. Perhaps some, black and white, wondered how I could be so even-keeled, and perhaps some, white as well as black, wanted me to be angrier. Some whites, in particular, appeared to think I should act, through my anger, as their conscience. The problem was that I already had a job—I did not have time to be anyone's conscience—and *there is a word for one who does others' work for no pay* (and I'm not thinking of "intern"). And so my beliefs, at bottom, held steady.

And then came the election of Donald Trump.

For a black man who has based his life on a belief in treating everyone as an individual and on an identification with America, what is the right response to a successful presidential campaign that brought out xenophobia like lava from a volcano? How do I respond to the fact that the majority of white voters, whom I have refused to hate as a group, supported this man? Should I hold on even tighter to the notion of being an American and fight to protect myself and my country from this menace? Or should I distance myself from a country where so many people seem to have demonstrated that they care nothing about me? Is it time to resign my post as the only nonracist black person in America? Or is now—when my principles are sorely tested—the most crucial time to hold on to them?

I had arrived at my beliefs with the help of Baldwin and Murray. But I began to sense during this crisis that I needed still another writer—not to give me answers, but to serve as a model for how I might find them on my own.

* * *

This writer puts me in mind—if this comparison is not too odd—of 1970s TV detectives, the kind with distinguishing characteristics; only instead of being old like Barnaby Jones, or overweight like Cannon, or a paraplegic like Ironside, or blind like Longstreet, or rumpled like Columbo, this writer-detective has characteristics you can't see at a glance, and her show, if she had one, would be highly unusual indeed. This writer-detective is a woman, yes, but her distinctiveness doesn't even begin there. She is glamorous—wearing dark glasses and dark, shoulder-length hair, holding a cigarette in long, elegant fingers—but her thinness and vague air of uncertainty and sadness also make her seem frail. All of that is odd enough in a detective, but it would be during the show's climax that we would see what truly makes her special. This is the part of every program when the detective reveals what really happened, who did the deed and why. As our detective begins to explain, we are struck by the length of her sentences: we think they're about to end, then realize they're just getting started, cohering perfectly for all their complexity and gathering force as they go; they have great power, these sentences, the force and sweep of a flood — but just as a flood is an awesome force carrying along all manner of small objects, these sentences, for all their epic proportions, are full of telling details. And yet even this isn't the astounding part. More startling than the power of our detective's phrasing is what she actually says, which is the opposite of what TV detectives usually say. The mystery, she tells us, gazing straight into the camera, will remain a mystery — because despite all she has learned about it, which is more than most would have uncovered, there are some things that no one knows or ever can know, secrets that a few are privy to but the rest of us never will be. Are you confused by what you've seen and heard, feeling somehow that it lacks logic or a point? Then, says the detective, you and I together have arrived at the same truth.

Who is this writer, this un-detective, this well-informed, tragic figure telling us that the more we learn, the less we know? She is Joan Didion.

It was because of my own writing that I began to investigate Didion's work. In the 1990s, around the time I started a family, I also began to write essays — many of them published in *The Threepenny Review* — that discussed books, jazz, film, and painting in relation to my own life, essays that mixed the personal with the critical, which I didn't see anyone else doing quite the same way. Here, it seemed, was the purpose of all my obsessive reading, all my late-night sessions of listening to classic jazz after putting the girls to bed, all my mad scribbling of previously unknown film titles, book titles, album titles in my ever-present pocket notebook. Writing about jazz, in particular, became a way of writing about life's challenges, and a few years later those pieces, along with personal essays and pieces on books and film, race and identity, made their way into my first book.

But how much is truly original? Whatever innovations I may have brought to the form, I knew I wasn't the first writer to inject personal elements into criticism and journalism or vice-versa; and so, wanting to explore what my forebears had done, I began a serious reading of the so-called New Journalists with whose works I was casually acquainted. I checked out books by Gay Talese and Hunter S. Thompson; I read quite a bit of Norman Mailer's nonfiction and everything written up to that time by Tom Wolfe (a piece on Wolfe would appear in my first book). But as much as I enjoyed Wolfe's similes and smart-assedness, Talese's calm eloquence, Thompson's wackiness, and Mailer's sheer ego, there was one writer among this crowd whose work, for me, surpassed the rest.

More than any of the others, Joan Didion's essays gave me the sense — for all that some call her inscrutable — of revealing the person behind them, of letting the reader in, as suggested by her oft-repeated phrase "I want to tell you about..." And once, in assessing the character of the artist Georgia O'Keeffe, she might have been talking instead about herself — "a woman clean of received wisdom and open to what she sees."

Didion's work appealed to me for other reasons, too. Her sadness, her flirtations with a sense of meaninglessness, spoke to something in me. I had, I supposed, also reached what the novelist Jane Smiley calls the "age of grief," one that perhaps every parent, deep in his or her heart, comes to eventually. In 2006 my wife, my daughters, and I vacationed at a lake house in Maine with two other couples and their young children. The setting was gorgeous, the water clear, the air pleasantly crisp and filled with our kids' joyous shouts; here was the kind of atmosphere that ought to have inspired me, even if it inspired only my contented sighs, but also the kind that can sometimes point up, by contrast, what is wrong. "Usually such beautiful landscapes fill me with a sense of possibility," I wrote in my journal during that vacation, in an entry dated August 25, 2006; I went on to note my "old sadness/sense of pointlessness, esp. as regards the kids — sadness *for* them, a feeling of futility *for* them." Watching my girls running around outside and having fun with the other kids, which should have made me happy, only gave me the feeling that in the end their earnest, heartbreaking efforts to do, learn, and grow would pass into oblivion along with their childhoods, would amount to — what? — in a big world that wouldn't love my children the way I did. In the journal entry, written more than a decade ago now, I can feel my effort to comfort myself, as when I wrote, "[T]he past isn't past. The good memories of childhood (just like the bad ones) are with you always. NOTHING is FUTILE, in life or art." I needed to hold on to something, clearly. The first sentence of Didion's essay "The White Album" comes to mind: "We tell ourselves stories in order to live."

I was trying to allay my worries, but I wonder now if the true cause of those worries about my daughters was that they were being raised and protected, in this mean, mean world, by...*me*? Surely those wonderful girls deserved someone smarter, stronger, more capable? The happier my children seemed, the sadder their plight appeared to me, those poor kids blind to the shakiness of their lives' foundations. Somehow — and so far — those girls, now young women, have survived despite having a father who managed to pass the age of fifty without getting it through his skull what his country really thinks of him. *Or is now — when my principles are sorely tested — the most crucial time to hold on to them?* Or is this very question a desperate attempt to evade the ugly truth? Is it worse, as twilight approaches, to be a fool or to turn my back on what makes me who I am?

In this dark hour, it is the quality of Didion's that she observed in Georgia O'Keeffe — being "clean of received wisdom and open to what she sees" — that I most need to take on as my own. Given recent events, given daily affirmation that the country I have chosen to identify with has chosen a racist as its leader, how do I continue to live in the only place I have ever called home? To know, it is necessary to take a clear-eyed look at that place, and at myself, as Didion has so many times, and to be open to what I see there, whether or not it is what I hope to find.

If anyone seems to understand the problem of getting through one's life without even the most basic knowledge of how, it is Didion. In "The White Album," Didion wrote about her seemingly normal functioning during a period of profound personal confusion, "This was an adequate enough performance, as improvisations go. The only problem was that my entire education, everything I had ever been told or had told myself, insisted that the production was never meant to be improvised: I was supposed to have a script, and had mislaid it. I was supposed to hear cues, and no longer did."

The irony here is that if Didion felt she lacked the ability, in her life, to improvise — that ability at the heart of jazz — her writing is absolutely jazzlike. In her sentences, phrases riff on one another ("tells us something interesting about ourselves, something only dimly remembered, tells us that…"); long dependent clauses explore ideas suggested by main clauses, as the work of a jazz horn player explores chords undergirding melody; and in her investigations of topics, Didion gets to the heart of things without knowing beforehand what is there, where she is going; she goes in with her eyes open to what she will find, and she responds accordingly, like a jazz musician responding to what his bandmates are playing, acting in the moment.

Now, aching over my empty nest and contemplating the world around me, it is the improvisatory skill and doggedness of the jazz musician and the clear sight of Joan Didion that I hope to bring to this book. Through travel and the one-on-one interviews recorded here, I have even tried to emulate the way Didion sets out to see, for herself, not what is in her own head but what is really going on.

Clifford Thompson
January 2018

One

I refer often in this book to "rootedness." What I mean by that word is a sense of stability and security based on identification with an entity or idea, a condition that most humans seek, not always consciously, the way water seeks its own level. Rootedness gives us a feeling of belonging, of being part of something greater than ourselves. It often provides the lens through which we view the world, sometimes making us unable to see what is in front of our eyes.

The ways that I was rooted for the first eighteen years of my life were determined largely by where I grew up. I was born in 1963 and lived for my entire childhood in a semidetached red brick house in Washington, DC, in a neighborhood that was totally black. As far as I know, no adult in our neighborhood ever started a conversation with her child by saying, "This place is special because..."

But there were certainly things that made us who we were. There was crime, but there was also an unspoken trust; we routinely left our front and back doors open during warm weather to let in the breeze—along with the sounds of cicadas and the lazy roar of the occasional car going up the street—not worried about who might come walking in. People sometimes *did* come walking in, but they were mostly neighbors, who, in my case, were also relatives—my mother's aunt and uncle, my father's sisters and their husbands, who like my parents and many of my friends' parents had made their way to DC from farther south, bringing their flat vowels and folksiness. If you were walking down the street in my neighborhood and passed someone, you both spoke, even if you didn't know each other. There was no need to avoid certain blocks because the people there didn't like your kind; *everybody* was your kind, everybody was black—your teachers, your classmates, the people you sat next to on the 40 bus heading out on East Capitol Street, the people standing in line at the Safeway at the corner of Division Avenue Northeast and Nannie Helen Burroughs.

My memory is selective—the selection process based on no logic I can fathom—but is also, when it works, long and sharp. I remember, for example, a conversation with a counselor at the summer day camp I attended for five years running; the counselor was asking, for some reason, about my family's socioeconomic status, and he concluded, based on what I said, that we were "lower upper-middle-class," with which I agreed. That makes me laugh now. On a clear day, with binoculars, no one in my neighborhood could have seen so much as the sagging bottom of the upper middle class. But my response to the counselor reflected, if not my actual circumstances, then my never having been deprived of anything, as far as I knew. And indeed, by the standards of the neighborhood, we were pretty well-off. Our house was certainly small — I spent years of my early childhood sharing a bedroom with my grandmother and two much older sisters — but we *had* a house, complete with a backyard and a basement, unlike the residents of the two housing projects that sandwiched our block, one of which was home to most of my friends. On the other hand, I remember as a teenager passing the open door of my widowed mother's bedroom, where she sat on the edge of the bed crying, because she wanted braces for me and had been told they would cost between one and three thousand dollars — which, on her salary as a postal clerk on the night shift, she couldn't have begun to afford.

As a kid, then, I was not rich any way you looked at it, but, leaving aside the normal stresses of childhood, I did not suffer hardship. I lived in a nurturing environment, and many of my memories are good ones. To this hour, when I can't sleep, I picture the view from one of the windows at the back of the house; I see the tree in our backyard, through whose limbs and branches slivers of the Lincoln Heights housing project's red brick are visible; in the summer at dusk, when the sky is that special, fleeting pastel blue and the breeze caresses the limbs just so, the leaves sway, as if moving to a slow tune I can't hear.

Everybody in our neighborhood was not only black but Christian, too, so I was a Christian. In our family, unlike some on our block, we did not put on our best clothes on Sunday morning, pile into the car together, and drive off to spend half the day in church. My parents were believers, though, and while we didn't go to church as a family when I was little, my siblings made their way there individually—my older brother to a Baptist church, one of my sisters to the local Catholic church. People's surprise at that makes me chuckle, because they assume there must have been some acrimonious Catholic/Protestant split in my family, when the truth is that having a Catholic and a Protestant under the same roof was no more significant to us than it would have been elsewhere to have blonds and brunettes in the same classroom. The only real division was between Christians and non-Christians, of whom we knew none. When I was fourteen and my mother decided that she and I should start going to church and get baptized, she chose the Catholic church my sister attended, mainly, I think, because it was closest. I went along with this happily enough. I was never fervently religious, but I drew some comfort from faith. I can remember thinking that if my mother died anytime soon, I would be very sad, but it would be okay in the end—I would see her in heaven.

So there was rootedness in blackness, in religion, in the ways that rural folks brought to the city. And then there was one way that my family, in particular, was rooted, a way that actually did get discussed. I think it applied to our whole family, but it was especially true of one of my sisters.

I may have been eight. Phyllis and I were walking home from somewhere; ten and a half years my senior, the youngest of my siblings and the last of them to leave the nest, she often took me with her to various places around the city and in the neighborhood. It was warm out, as I recall, and we were coming down the hill of Division Avenue, our street, passing houses that were small but freestanding, built atop grassy mounds, different from one another, unlike the uniform semidetached brick houses of our block. I don't remember how the conversation started, but at one point I said, "They hate us." By "they," I meant white people.

Phyllis responded, calmly. Because she was so much older and taller than me, her words came to me from above, literally and otherwise. "Just remember they're not all the same," she said, or words very much like that, "just like we're not all the same."

So: our family was not antiwhite. I hasten to add that we didn't think white people were special or better than we were; it was simply that we were against prejudice toward *anyone*. The thinking, I would say, went more or less this way: if racism was the cause of black people's problems, then racism was the very last thing that a black person, in particular, should embrace. A person was a person, and unless that specific person had wronged you, there was no reason to treat him or her with less than the respect that was due any human being.

My family and I were certainly not unaware of, or indifferent to, white racism. The comment I made at eight about white people ("They hate us") was obviously inspired by *something*, some observation or overheard exchange I could only make wild guesses about now. But generally speaking, I, at least, had the sense during that era — the early 1970s, when my awareness of the world was taking shape — that things were much better for black people than they had been in a time I couldn't remember. Martin Luther King Jr. had been assassinated just a few years earlier, part of what I now understand was a backlash against the civil rights era, but I didn't consider his murder as proof of the folly of hope any more than Christians looked on Christ's crucifixion as a reason to suspend their faith in God. King had died for our people, and we were in a new day. It was not that I thought the world was the same place for me that it was for a white boy. During my twenties I had a conversation with a guy, white and Jewish, with whom I was friends at the time; he told me he remembered his elementary school teacher crying over Watergate. When I asked "Why was she crying?" he seemed surprised, and said, "Well, I think common sense would tell you — she felt disillusioned that people running the country would do what they did." Actually, for someone who grew up in my neighborhood, common sense would indicate no such thing. To be disillusioned, one must first have illusions, and when it came to the US government, we had precious few. But we did have a sense of hope, or I did. My parents had not been to college, but all three of my siblings had, and I took it for granted that I would go, too. I never doubted my chances for success. The world was not perfect, but I meant to live in it, treating others with openness and respect until they gave me a reason not to.

Nearly half a century later, that belief remains one of the pillars of my thinking. But like an actual pillar that has been exposed to the world for that long, it has seen things get messy around it.

College undid some — much — of my rootedness. I was certainly no longer in an all-black environment; Oberlin College, where I enrolled in 1981, had three thousand students, of whom maybe two hundred were black. Then there was Christianity. I am hardly unique in having lost my Christian faith at some point during my college years; the late novelist Maeve Binchy, I recall for some reason, took a trip as a young woman to Israel, where she saw the site of the Last Supper — a trip that seems to have had the opposite of its intended effect — and later told an interviewer about the experience, "One moment I believed the lot, angels with wings and a special Irish God, and the next I didn't believe a word of it." I don't remember an experience like Binchy's, a single instance of thinking, "You know, I just don't believe this stuff anymore." All I know is that I entered college believing that Jesus had died for my sins and left four years later not believing anything at all. I remember telling a co-worker when I was around twenty-four, "I believe in the possibility of everything." That is more or less where I stand now.

I think of the time, in 2000, when my 106-year-old maternal grandmother lay dying in my sister's house. A visiting nurse told my sister to watch the cat that was hanging around my grandmother's bed; when the cat fled the room, it would be because our grandmother had passed away. The nurse had seen this a hundred times. What was the cat running from? I am not offering a guess — merely citing this as an example of things that are hard to explain according to what we currently understand. As I once heard it put: *All I can say for sure is that I don't know.* And I don't know how anyone else can know, either. So I find committed atheists a bit arrogant, though not as arrogant as those who cite their knowledge of God's will in saying that you and your sex partner should not have matching genitalia.

This, however, must be said for Christianity: in its purest form, as opposed to its frequent role as a political weapon and a justification for all sorts of exclusion and worse, it is based on an idea—love for our fellow humans—with which only the truly hard-hearted could find fault. When one considers the state of the world, the terrible things people do to one another every day despite technology that has so much potential for good, one has to be amazed that two thousand years ago, people who lived in the most rudimentary of ways, who lived "poor, nasty, brutish, and short" lives, in Thomas Hobbes' famous words, conceived of a philosophy based on the very highest of human ideals. And there is something beautiful—I write this without facetiousness or condescension—in choosing to believe in the symbol of these ideals, choosing a faith that flies in the face of all evidence and is perhaps made, for the faithful, all the more vital by that very fact.

But I will return to this idea later—much later—and, again, I was speaking of rootedness. After I left the place where I grew up, I was no longer rooted in an all-black environment, and yet, while that source of rootedness was no more, my having had it helped to reaffirm another source: my opposition to prejudice. Consider this: some of the most vehement of black separatists I met in college were those who had grown up and gone to school in integrated environments. In their formative and most impressionable years, in other words, they raised their bony brown arms in class, trying to answer teachers' questions; took tentative steps into the social scene of the cafeteria, tightly and nervously clutching brown paper bags or lunch trays; got their Levi's and sweatshirts muddy and their faces and necks shiny with sweat on the football field; and stood in front of mirrors before setting off to those horrible dances — all in the company of white kids, who, not because they are white but because they are kids, are the meanest people on God's Earth, people without filters, people who do all manner of cruel things to one another and who will say, literally, anything. I could make guesses all day about how I would have been affected as a boy by taunts from mean-assed white kids, about how such abuse would or would not have shaped me, but I will never know. Before the age of eighteen, having gotten to know virtually no white kids, I hadn't had an opportunity to dislike them, and by the time I met them, they were all eighteen or older, too. That is not to say that they had been shorn of insensitivity or the potential for racism; it *is* to say that I was meeting them after they had developed enough sophistication to be admitted to a very good college with a reputation for liberalism, that I was meeting their improved selves, the people they became after the era of schoolyard taunts was over. And my grounding in a solidly black environment, ironically, made me open to them.

This rootedness in opposition to prejudice gave me something of a sense of superiority. I hung out with white kids I met in a dorm I had chosen randomly, and I even had the temerity — mainly because it didn't occur to me to consider it that — to date one of them; when I emerged from my bubble long enough to register that other black students disapproved of all this, their attitudes bothered me but did not pierce me to the core, because I felt superior to such attitudes, believing that prejudice — all prejudice — was small-minded and simply wrong. And I could not imagine ever feeling differently.

Generally speaking, though, as I entered my twenties, I felt my sense of rootedness — which I had taken for granted, as one takes for granted the ground beneath one's feet — to be giving way. I no longer lived exclusively or even primarily among blacks, so that source of rootedness was no more. Similarly, I no longer had the comfort of religion. My beliefs in "the possibility of everything" and in the rightness of treating everyone as an individual — the latter reinforced by Baldwin's writing — still made sense to me, but after a time they began to seem pretty thin soil in which to root oneself. My white friends, God bless them, never questioned the way I lived, which could not be said for some of the blacks I knew; these white friends simply let me be myself — and yet, as I laughed and joked in their presence, sitting next to them amid the din of bars or drinking beer from the bottle while standing among clusters of them at one of those countless, dimly remembered parties from my twenties, sometimes a voice whispered, somehow very audibly in those loud gatherings, that I was alone.

Then came my discovery of Albert Murray's work, with its emphasis on the integral place of blacks in

America, a legacy of grit, resourcefulness, accomplishment, and improvisation, all symbolized by that signature cultural contribution, jazz, my beloved jazz — and all at once, I felt rootless no more. I felt an invisible barrier between me and others, one I had only dimly perceived, melt away; and I relaxed in a way I never had as an adult.

If anything, I became a little too rooted in Murray's sensibility, in a way that blinded me to what was going on.

I got to know Murray personally when I profiled him in 1994 for *Current Biography*, a publication of the reference-book company where I worked then. (I later became *Current Biography*'s editor in chief.) From then until Murray's death, in 2013, at age ninety-seven, I was an occasional guest at his book-filled apartment on West 132nd Street in Harlem. Murray greatly admired, as did I, those who fought against white racism, and he had a special place of reverence, as did I, for Martin Luther King Jr. But to paraphrase Murray in his book *The Blue Devils of Nada*: to fight dragons is heroic; to protest the existence of dragons is naïve. In his books and in person, Murray often expressed disdain for those blacks and other minorities who, you might say, purposely led with their chins — placing their status as victims at the center of their art or other work, making the value of that work *depend* on victimhood, protesting the existence of the dragons without which their work would have no meaning.

I developed my own disdain for what I privately called the Victim Elite. This was the all-but-official membership of those who cherished their grievances, stroking them like pampered cats, erecting temples to their own alienation, temples founded every bit as much on exclusion as any southern good old boys' club. Theirs was the kind of thinking that mimicked exclusion instead of fighting it, that led, for example, Terry McMillan to say to the *New York Times* in 1992, in reference to John Updike's quartet of novels about Harry "Rabbit" Angstrom, "Who gives a [expletive] about Rabbit?" Well, I did — I happened to love those books. Theirs was the kind of thinking that made them unable to (rightly) champion works outside the white male canon without trashing everything within that canon, sight unseen, along with anyone who had anything positive to say about it. Theirs was the kind of thinking that let them see no irony in the generalities they made with such abandon, dismissals of whole segments of the population — whites, men, heterosexuals. And theirs was the kind of thinking that led to an exchange I had one day in the mid-1990s. I belonged for a couple of years during that period to a small writing group that met in Park Slope diners and coffee shops. We traded work (all fiction) and sometimes passed around works by established writers that we had found interesting or useful. One week I gave the others a short story I'd written as well as the story that had inspired it: "You Can't Tell a Man by the Song He

Sings," from Philip Roth's collection *Goodbye, Columbus*, an early, short work infused with elements that attract me to his writing as a whole: the shock of recognition at his characters' quirks and contradictions, the passages that make me laugh aloud. With the two other people who showed up that week—both women—I discussed my story, then tried to talk about the Philip Roth piece. One of the women made a few observations about it; the other simply said, "I didn't read Philip." It was not those four words that ended the conversation but their tone: hard and dry, like four gray granite walls of a closed-off room containing fixed, unchangeable ideas. It didn't matter that the unspoken rules of our little group obligated her to read the things that other members passed along; it didn't matter that another member of the group had seen something of value in this short story and thought that she and others might, too. Her unwillingness to risk being made uncomfortable as a reader and her preconceived notions about Roth—what some assumed, from his fiction, to be his negative attitude toward women—overrode the rules of our writing group, and so she *didn't read Philip*.

That kind of thinking still drives me crazy. But I now think that my contempt for the fetishization of victimhood interfered with my ability to tell the difference between such self-righteous xenophobia and legitimate complaint. To put it as plainly as possible: I was a good man with a blind spot. I was never indifferent to white racism, and I don't want to suggest that I ever was; all the attention paid during that period to Charles Murray's idiotic book *The Bell Curve*, for example, with its nineteenth-century-style theories about race and intelligence, nearly made blood come out of my nose. I was not unaware that racism continued to plague the black community. And yet. I understood that black children in poor neighborhoods faced disadvantages from the word go, and I knew about racism in everything from housing to employment to the legal system to environmental health; I knew that kind of racism needed to be fought; I knew it was behind the need to sell drugs, which was behind a lot of the violence. And yet. With no concrete evidence to go on, I wondered if black people should be doing something to help ourselves, something central and crucial, something that had little to do with white racism, that we weren't doing.

But in any case, there it was: my particular rootedness, which gave me a sense of connectedness to my heritage, allowed me to continue exploring the works of other cultures while feeling secure in my own culture, made me able to operate in the world with confidence, and made me, deep inside, maybe just a little self-satisfied.

But there was trouble in paradise.

Two

Trouble often arises from contradiction. There are those contradictions you can live with, and those you can't.

One of the former, for me, is having children. I mention being a father not because it makes me special—it hardly does that—but because it makes me representative. Parenthood has given me, all at once and paradoxically, an appreciation for the fragility and preciousness of life, a sense of inadequacy in my role as shepherd of two young lives, and a tendency to wonder what life—all life—is for.

How can I feel all of that at once? Let me begin answering that by telling you a story about my wife. Amy grew up in Manhattan with her younger siblings, a sister and a brother. When she was five years old, her mother underwent a gallbladder operation. The operation was botched. From then on Amy's mother was mostly bedridden. Her father, a book editor at the publishing house where he had met Amy's mother, took up the slack where the care of his family was concerned—until, that is, he got lung cancer, which acted on him very quickly. Amy was eleven when he died. For the next six years her mother was in and out of the hospital. Amy was seventeen when her mother, too, passed away. For her senior year of high school, she was taken in by the family of a classmate, while her sister and brother went to Maryland to live a Dickensian existence with their mother's sister and her family—adding feelings of guilt to Amy's other troubles.

Amy, slender and blond, has a way about her that I don't think is unconnected to the events of her childhood. She is a caring person, utterly devoted to her family and friends, she loves a good laugh, but politeness is not her bag. She can be frank in a way that some find startling. We make, in some ways, an odd pair. I grew up in a family that was polite to the point of indecisiveness. ("What do you want to do?" "Doesn't matter, whatever you like.") Amy cuts through all that. She knows what she wants, and she tells you what it is. Maybe in life we seek out the people who supply what we are missing. In any case, I've always seen her manner as following at least partially from the events of her formative years and the lessons she took from them. *Life is short and unpredictable. We don't have the luxury of dithering.* She has an air of knowing what to do. I admire it. Sometimes it drives me a little crazy. And she never breaks my heart more, this woman I love, than in those rare times when that quality of hers falters.

Which brings me to our children. Amy is a terrific mother — maybe the best one I know — but if there are times when neither of us knows what to do, it is because the job of parenting involves fundamental contradictions. There is, for example...

The disconnect between your necessary efforts and the way things turn out. Our younger daughter is, today, a quiet, truly sweet young woman. As a baby, she could cry like nothing and no one you ever heard. Oh, my Lord, could she cry. I'm thinking of one summer night in our apartment in the late 1990s; our daughter — let's call her by one of her nicknames, Louie — was maybe a year old, maybe a little younger. For whatever reason, and Amy and I nearly drove ourselves insane trying to figure out what it was, on this night Louie simply would not stop crying. Her eyes were slits of misery, her mouth in the shape of a mangled wheel, and good God, the noise she made. Imagine the wails that would come out of you if a rusty nail was slowly inserted into your pupil, and imagine those wails playing on a loop, and you begin to have some idea of what she sounded like, on and on into the night. Someone outside may have thought that's what we were doing to her, because in the middle of this madness, through the open bathroom window of our third-floor apartment, I somehow heard — during one of those rare, blessed pauses in Louie's shrieking — a young male nitwit who was standing at the bus stop call up toward us in a singsong, "Ba-by...why's the baby crying?" *"Because she's a baby, ya moron!*" I yelled back. He must have called the cops; the next day a downstairs neighbor told us that the police had come to the door but left upon being reassured that all was well. Our upstairs neighbor, meanwhile, lost his patience — I distinctly heard him shout, *"Jesus!"* — and the whole time, Amy and I were passing Louie back and forth, jiggling her, cooing at her, feeling more and more desperate, resisting the urge to toss our daughter and then ourselves out the window. Finally, Amy, who was holding her, could take no more. Now my wife *and* my daughter were crying, and seeing Amy's usual air of assuredness break down, I wanted to cry, too. Instead, I said, "Here, I'll take her." While Amy went to try to sleep, I held Louie and willed her to stop crying. And she stopped.

Needless to say, she didn't stop because I willed her to. She stopped on her own. And there you have it. You try, and try, and try, and if you're lucky things turn out okay, but not necessarily because you exhausted yourself trying, and that, in a nutshell, is parenthood. And those are just the times when you try as hard as you should. Then there are the other times, when, despite your best intentions, you find yourself asleep at the switch, because, in the end . . .

You are not equal to this job you must do. In my memoir *Twin of Blackness*, I referred to Louie's older sister by one of the nicknames she had as a little kid: The Pie. Let's keep calling her that. One Saturday in the winter of, I think, 2000, when The Pie was about six, she and I bundled up and walked a block to Prospect Park so she could sled. The park was frozen over, all white and silver and glistening in the January sun, and packed with families. I don't know what my excuse is — I don't know if I have one — for what happened next; maybe I was sleep-deprived from being up during the night with Louie. In any case, I took The Pie to the top of a hill, she got in her plastic sled, and soon she was flying toward the bottom — before I took in what was down there, jutting up out of the whiteness: a big, hard tree, and, a few yards away from the tree lengthwise and widthwise, a black cast-iron lamppost. When I saw the tree and the lamppost, I also saw that my daughter was heading right for them. I ran after her, helplessly, footfalls crunching in the snow, shouting her name, with as much chance of catching her as of catching a runaway train. She picked up speed as she headed for the tree and the pole. And then…she sailed right between them. She was fine, no thanks to me — in spite of me. I don't think a week has passed since that I haven't remembered that episode, and when I'm in the mood to torture myself, I imagine an alternate ending, the one I deserved for letting my guard down, as I always feared I would. Of course, even when you don't let your guard down, even when you do what you mean to do, you wonder if it's the right thing, because…

Your impulses often go against your mission. I think, too, about one day when Louie was about three years old and I took her to another kid's birthday party. The kids played musical chairs, one of the many games devised by adults to torture children. After one of the rounds, Louie came toddling toward where I was sitting, and I'll never forget the way she looked. This was the face of a little girl who had had enough of the rough-and-tumble, whose defenses were worn down, who simply needed, if only for a minute or two, to be held. I've met parents who would have told their kids in that moment to just toughen up and get back in the game, in preparation for a life without their dads to comfort them. Maybe that would have been the right thing to do. But I took Louie onto my lap. Father and daughter, wusses together. Sometimes, in other words, you make mistakes not because you don't love your kids but because you do. They become the center of your world, in fact. And then...

After all that, they leave you. This is as it should be, though I will say that I got a glimpse of the pulling-away process that no father should ever get. One warm weekday evening when The Pie was no longer a six-year-old on a sled but a sophomore at a Manhattan high school, she hung out with friends in the city. Then she rode the subway back to Brooklyn and called me from the station to let me know she was on the way home. Reassured, I went back to my book or newspaper. Fifteen or twenty minutes later, I realized she should have been home by now—the walk from the subway was no more than ten minutes. After another ten or fifteen minutes had passed, I decided to go outside and see if I could spot her. I walked out of the apartment building, hung a right, went to the corner, and looked down the avenue, where-upon I had the following sequence of thoughts:

Oh, good, there she is.

Oh, okay, she's hugging her friend goodbye.

Oh.

She parted from the young man — her first real boy-friend — and walked toward me. We looked at each other sheepishly, then went, without a word, into our building.

And that, of course, was just the beginning of the pulling-away process, which brings me back to the hope-lessly unoriginal yet persistent question of what it's all for. You and your partner, or you alone, work to build a family; you worry, and you worry some more, every day, until one day your children are grown and (you hope) capable human beings; and then they leave, off (you hope) to become productive members of society, to do their part in sustaining that society, leaving you with a hole in your heart — and that's when things go well! Your chil-dren may start their own families and produce society-sustaining adults, sweating over their children so those children can grow up and leave and maybe start families, and on, and on, and... why? What *is* this society, that our children must leave us to maintain it, that its mainte-nance requires of us such trial and heartbreak, requires that we deny our laps to our toddlers? (And doing so may make them more ready to face the world, but might it not also make them just a little colder?) I could be accused here of protesting the existence of dragons, but I don't think that's it; as everyone surely does from time to time, I simply, honestly, wonder. In any case, these are the contradictions of parenthood—being told (1) This is your vital mission; (2) You are not equipped to carry out this mission; (3) This mission, like everything surrounding it, makes no sense; (4) Go!

And of course you go, because that is simply what you do. All parenting is the same, and each job of parenting brings its unique challenges. My daughters, whose mother is white, look pretty different from me. They don't quite look white, but you wouldn't look at them and think "black," either. This bothered me in the very beginning, not because I could not see blackness in them but because I could not see *me* in them, which went against that biological drive that produces children in the first place: the blind desire to continue the species, to recreate oneself. But our bond quickly overrode any doubts. These children were mine; that was all. Of course, what one knows and what the world sees are different. With rare exceptions, such as the homeless man who saw me walking with Louie and said "Y'all look just alike!," strangers see me next to my daughters, who have white girls' hair and skin much lighter than mine, and they are thrown, here in the twenty-first century, for a loop. A college friend of mine, a black man who visits me in New York once a year or so, walked beside me one day as I pushed Louie in a stroller and observed about the people passing us: "The white people have looks on their faces like, 'Oh, okay.' The black people are like, 'Uh-*huh*.'" A white cabdriver in upstate New York, who picked up Amy, Louie, and me, came out and asked us, "Are you guys a family?" I could not love my daughters a bit more if they were mirror images of me; I could not love them any more than I do now. Amy and I have tried to teach them to be kind people. Whether or not because of that, they are kind people. I have talked to them about their black American heritage; when they were younger, I often mentioned to them the African kingdoms of Mali, Ghana, and the Songhai (I don't know if they remember); God knows I've played them a lot of jazz. For the most part, though, their identities, cultural and otherwise, are theirs to figure out. I have done what I knew how to do. That is what most parents do for their children.

All this is to say that parenthood comprises a set of screaming contradictions that you somehow learn to live with. And then there are those contradictions that simply stop you in your tracks, that pit all you believe and all you are against the reality in front of you.

One such contradiction was revealed, for me, by the election of Donald Trump. That catastrophe does have one factor in common with parenthood: it has forced me to consider things anew. (And the two were to lead me to similar conclusions in the end... but I will come to that.)

Life is complex, and results often have more than one cause. While Trump's election made me aware that I was rethinking things, the process had probably been set in motion earlier, and by other factors.

Let's recall the elements of my brand of rootedness. I came from a family who believed in judging others, in Martin Luther King's famous phrase, not by the color of their skin, but by the content of their character; in my early thirties, after a season spent intellectually and culturally at sea, I declared myself to be an American, to be one with my fellow countrymen of every shade, based on my particular people's contributions to our nation. But life is complex, and even as I made that declaration — and even as I wondered how many problems facing black people we could simply solve ourselves — there were things that could not escape the notice of even a head-in-the-clouds sort of guy like me.

When it comes to experiencing racism, I have been luckier than many black people. Please know that I know that. Part of that is living in New York City and not owning a car; I am not guilty of Driving While Black on anything like a regular basis. But I have suffered the indignities that are as common among black Americans as tap water. Let a couple of examples stand for the rest:

In the fall of 1990 I lived with Amy in her studio apartment in Park Slope. One night when she was coming home by herself from an outing, I went to meet her at the subway station. As I was leaving our apartment building, it seemed to me that the front door wasn't closing properly, and I tried to get it to lock behind me. After either succeeding or giving up—I don't remember which—I kept on my way, exchanging glances with a white guy who was coming in as I was heading out. I met Amy at the station, and we walked back home together. Approaching our building, I saw the guy who had glanced at me as I left; he was still in front of the door, only now he was talking to two white police officers. Seeing me, and looking bewildered, the guy said to the cops, "It's him." The cops sized up the situation and left, one of them laughing and clapping me on the shoulder as he walked away. The cop's laughter — which broke the tension, which appeared to mark the moment when the episode turned from serious to comic, which introduced a welcome human element to this encounter, suggesting that it could be forgotten — now seems to me the most depressing part of it all. *You were just minding your business,* this laugh seemed to say, *and this race thing fucked with you anyway.* Yes, isn't that hilarious? *What can you do but laugh,* this laugh suggested, *since this is just how it is?* — "it" obviously being beyond the control of mere mortals. This laughter, so easy for that white cop, amounted to a pronouncement of my fate.

That, anyway, is how I hear it now. At the time, this episode seemed to be of the kind that passes quickly and without apparent harm, fading with others like it into the recesses of memory, like an afternoon here and there spent sunbathing — until the day you discover that you have skin cancer.

It has been said that what we call "cancer" actually comprises many diseases, and, similarly, race-related aggravation — skin-color cancer, you might call it — comes in many forms. A decade or so ago, when I was rather lazily job-hunting, the brother of a white friend of mine passed along my resume via email to someone he knew. That email, which I saw, referred to me as, among other things, "reasonable." Do white people, I thought, refer to each other as "reasonable"? Or is this a code word for a black person who doesn't stir up trouble, which he might otherwise be assumed to make a habit of doing, given his skin color? And did everyone know this except me?

The examples went beyond—far beyond—my personal experiences, and they encompassed history as well as current events, the two gradually beginning to seem like one and the same thing. There was, for example, convict leasing: the practice in the South, after slavery was abolished, of locking up black people for "crimes" that included not moving out of the way of a white person on the sidewalk, then leasing these prisoners to mining companies to do work that could, and often did, kill them. *You were just minding your business, and this race thing fucked with you anyway.* This practice, slavery in everything but name, went on well into the twentieth century. It is over now, of course—the only problem being that it isn't.

Reading Michelle Alexander's 2010 book *The New Jim Crow* was either one of the best or one of the worst experiences of my life, but was, in any case, one of the most illuminating. Alexander leads her reader, without a trace of hysteria, patiently and step by logical step, to the unarguable conclusion that American criminal justice is not merely the imperfect, racially biased system some of us knew it to be but, rather, a free-roaming beast leaving untold numbers of ruined black and brown lives in its wake. To give a much-too-brief summary of Alexander's book: the War on Drugs, while based on laws ostensibly unrelated to race and therefore difficult to combat on those grounds, has not only freed police departments to pursue drug crimes any way they see fit—leaving the door open for rampant racial profiling—but has given police financial incentives for doing so. "Modern drug forfeiture laws date back to 1970 . . . ," Alexander writes. "But it was not until 1984, when Congress amended the federal law to allow federal law agencies to retain and use any and all proceeds from asset forfeitures, and to allow state and local police agencies to retain up to 80 percent of the assets' value, that a true revolution occurred." While, as Alexander points out, blacks and whites have been shown to use and sell drugs at nearly identical rates, the police overwhelmingly target black (and brown) offenders, who end up in for-profit prisons. (Think about that term for a moment.) "Who becomes a social pariah and excommunicated from civil society and who trots off to college bears scant relationship to the morality of crimes committed," Alexander writes. "Who is more blameworthy: the young black kid who hustles on the street corner, selling weed to help his momma pay the rent? Or the college kid who deals drugs out of his dorm room so that he'll have cash to finance his spring break?" Once convicted, the drug offender is subject, *for life*, to all kinds of legal discrimination—in everything from employment to housing to voting to public benefits. A substantial percentage of the population, disproportionately black and brown, has been effectively stripped of citizenship.

As a boy, as a younger man, I knew, as everyone knew, that there was widespread racism in our past and in our present; but as the years passed I began to *feel* what I had always known. I understood some attitudes in a way I hadn't before and had less patience with others. In my ears, the question "But don't you feel like things are better than they were?"—always, always posed by a white person—went from seeming merely innocuous and unimaginative to being downright maddening. *In some ways, no*, became my answer, but the deeper answer was itself a question: What are you actually saying? That as long as you can point to some measure of progress, however bad other things may be, we should all be satisfied? That the natural condition of black people is oppression, and for any alleviation of that oppression, we should be grateful?

In this new frame of mind, formed so gradually that I can identify points along its development but not its beginning, I looked back on some things with different eyes. There was, for example, the case of Marion Barry. I was a teenager in DC when Barry, a black man, was first elected as the city's mayor, in 1978. A dozen years later, as all the world learned, Barry was caught on camera—in an

FBI sting operation—smoking crack in a hotel room while trying to bed a woman who was not his wife. He went to prison, but then, upon his release, in 1992, he won a seat on the City Council, and two years after that, to the disbelief of the rest of the country, he was elected mayor again. As a DC native—even as one who had been in New York for eight years by then—I was embarrassed. I simply could not understand how so many people in the city that produced me could have returned this man to office, seemingly with no regard for how it looked from the outside. But I get it now. Barry, who died in 2014, always maintained that his fierce championing of black business in DC angered moneyed elites, and it is certainly possible to argue over how true that was and to what extent it was a factor in the FBI operation that (temporarily) brought him down. But what is not arguable is that Barry cared deeply for his mostly black constituents and that the agency that sent him to prison was the same one that killed the humanist-minded Black Panther leader Fred Hampton in cold blood and that, if it did not actually kill Martin Luther King—a substantial "if"—did everything in its power to discredit him. In the eyes of so many DC residents, not only was Barry a better man than those who had tried to ruin him, but an argument against reelecting Barry could seem naïve, if not worse—an act of siding with the oppressor, deliberately or otherwise. It is not necessary to excuse Barry's drug use to understand this point.

For the June 5–12, 2017, issue of the *New Yorker*, Philip

Roth wrote a short essay in which he explained his unhesitating identification with America and his reasons for calling himself not a Jewish American writer but simply an American writer. The American authors whose works he read as a boy, he wrote, were not Jewish, but just as importantly, if not more so, he was a boy during World War II, when the United States took on the evil forces that were out to destroy Roth's people. While Roth recognized the continued existence of anti-Semitism and racism, he was a proud member of a country that once fought so mightily for him. How I envied Roth in this regard. You could argue that Union troops in the Civil War fought against slavery, and you could point out that President Eisenhower federalized troops in the South to ensure that black children could attend previously all-white schools amid jeers, epithets, and worse from red-faced white southerners, except that (1) Abraham Lincoln prosecuted the Civil War to preserve the union rather than to abolish slavery, and (2) in both cases, the government was defending black people *against our fellow citizens*. A break-even proposition at best. And so blacks who have, like me, identified with America have done so via a much more circuitous route than the one Roth took, one that we followed not because of the actions of the United States government but often, and very much, in spite of them.

It's to our culture, not to our government, that we turn, the culture linked so inextricably to the broader nation and its people. But then you're forced to look at some of the people. As for those police officers, most of them white, who almost exclusively target black and brown citizens for drug offenses: at this point many of those officers are young enough to be my sons and daughters, people born well after the arrival of that "new day" that I, as a boy, understood us to be in.

Trayvon Martin. Eric Garner. Tamir Rice. Sandra Bland. Black Americans are, in sum, and simply, a people to whom different rules often apply. But if we have an attitude because of that, then we're not being... reasonable. And while I continued to feel personally that blacks should take the high road with regard to all this — that we should not be anti-white, that we should judge others as individuals — it began to anger me that we were *expected* to take it.

The effect of all this on me is analogous to a trivial thing that happened when I was in college. For a semester I lived next door to a guy named Carl, who was around six feet eight inches tall and quite a ways north of two hundred pounds. I was (and am) around five-eight, and at the time I weighed all of about one-thirty-five. One day Carl, in a playful mood, picked me up and began to turn me this way and that. I was nineteen years old, but I may as well have been three — that was how easily Carl turned me upside down and back again; it is the only time in my life I can remember when I was so physically disoriented that I knew that one direction was up, and knew one was down, but didn't know which was which.

Sometimes incidents of skin-color cancer operated on me in a similar way. I knew that I believed in judging people, no matter who they were, as individuals; and I knew that many blacks disliked and distrusted whites automatically. I knew that one of those positions made sense to me, and the other didn't. But there were moments when I did not know which was which. And while I mostly remained disgusted by the idea of there being different "teams" of Americans, there were moments — with all my white friends, living in my mostly white neighborhood — when I wondered if I'd spent my life suiting up for the wrong one.

These two opposing beliefs stemmed from different concepts of what it meant to be a right-thinking person. That meant, for me, being a *good* person, and a quality essential to being a good person was to remain free of prejudice — any prejudice. For many black people, to be a right-thinking individual meant to be a good *black* person, one who was concerned, first and foremost, about other blacks, whatever that might mean for nonblacks. While only one of those beliefs seemed right to me, I found myself able to understand, as I had not been able to at one point in my life, the appeal — or at least the logic — of the other one.

This turn in my thinking could be seen in an episode that played out on Facebook in late March of 2016. When ISIS claimed responsibility for three coordinated suicide bombings in Brussels, which killed more than thirty people and injured three hundred, quite a few of my Facebook friends changed their profile photos, in solidarity, to the image of the Belgian flag. One friend, an African American whom I have known since college and who has black nationalist leanings, had a different response. He wanted, as he wrote in his Facebook post, to remind anyone thinking of posting an image of Belgium's flag that that country had been quite busy in the Congo in the late nineteenth and early twentieth centuries. Under King Leopold II, Belgium forced natives to mine rubber and precious minerals in their own land, setting quotas of materials to be dug up by villages and punishing shortfalls with mutilation, amputation of hands and feet, and murder. Between 1885 and 1908, an estimated ten million Congolese died this way. I already knew this bit of history, but I was willing to bet that most of my Facebook friends did not. I also thought my friend had raised an interesting and important point. So I shared his post.

I should have anticipated what would follow, but I did not. Angry that I had used the occasion of human death, pain, and suffering to score a political point — and I have to admit they weren't exactly wrong — a number of people "unfriended" me on Facebook. My own wife was angry with me. And then there was my exchange with another friend, a white woman. I had known her in college and after; I had since lost touch with her but then reconnected on Facebook, and she frequently and enthusiastically responded to many of my posts. I knew that this friend had made a life in Europe and was raising a daughter there, but I forgot *where* she lived in Europe until she wrote me in response to my post about the Congo. She was "beyond bewildered" by my post, she wrote from her computer in Belgium, lamenting that I seemed to have become "radicalized." Perhaps it is not a coincidence that I have not heard from her since then. And perhaps this was the cost of my changing frame of mind.

That was the state of my thinking on the evening of Tuesday, November 8, 2016, as Amy and I sat in our living room with good friends who live two blocks away, with the TV tuned to the election returns and champagne chilling in the refrigerator — champagne that, as it turned out, we would not drink for months — ready to toast the election of the first female president of the United States. After a while our friends departed, too depressed to continue watching. Louie was away at college, in a Midwestern town where she cast her first-ever vote, expecting to be part of history; but The Pie, a college graduate, was in New York, staying with Amy and me while she looked for an apartment, and shortly after our friends left, she came home and sat with us on the sofa to watch the returns. As things went from unsettling to grim, my older daughter quietly cried. I didn't know what to say to her. We were watching as a man who had bragged about fondling women he had never met, who had received but not rejected the endorsement of the Ku Klux Klan, was elected president. He was the choice of the majority of whites, those people I refused to hate, in America, that land I called my home.

And *this* was analogous to another small thing that had once happened to me, which didn't seem small at the time. When Amy and I were still dating, before I moved into her studio in Park Slope, I had an apartment in Harlem. One weekday morning in 1990, after I had spent the night in the Slope, I returned to Harlem to find my apartment door ajar. With a sick feeling, I slowly pushed the door all the way open. Burglars had ransacked the place. My clothes had been tossed every which way, and my computer and television were gone, along with other items I've now forgotten but mourned the loss of then. What I now find interesting about that experience was my thought process at the time. I kept thinking that if I just looked hard enough in my apartment, searched every corner, racked my brain for where my stuff might be hiding, I would find it all.

This, of course, is called denial. And I felt the same impulse after Trump was elected. My mind, at first, refused to accept that this had happened. But slowly I acknowledged this truth, and I began to think about what it meant.

And I felt my roots loosening.

*　*　*

But I remembered what I mentioned in the Introduction to this book, the lesson taught by jazz musicians and by figures from the Underground Railroad and the civil rights movement: that when the way before you is not clear, or does not exist, you must make a way — you must, like Freddie Hubbard blowing those piercing trumpet notes through Art Blakey's thundering drum beats, go doggedly forward. You must improvise. I thought of the man who had been most important in passing that lesson on to me. I missed Albert Murray's counsel, missed sitting down to talk with him in his book-filled Harlem apartment, which mostly meant listening to him; and I thought of what he might say to me now, with his high voice and rapid speech. Tough times, he often said and wrote, offer "antagonistic cooperation," providing what every hero needs — something over which to triumph. I was, of course, feeling not like a hero but like a guy who was not getting any younger and whose bubble had belatedly burst. "That's part of the struggle," he might say at this point. "You think your ancestors didn't struggle? You think you've got it worse than they did?"

And of course I don't. But what if my ancestors were wrong? What if they struggled because they thought there was a promised land for their descendants, which they couldn't know we will never reach?

And, oh, I can imagine his response to that. "All the times you've been to see me, and you haven't learned any better than that? You're ready to give up all your ancestors struggled for just because some dumbass made it to the White House?"

But, of course, it's not just Trump that's the problem. It's all the people who voted for him—less than half the voters, but more than half of white voters.

And this imagined dialogue with my late mentor made me realize something: *Was I upset because that minority of voters who supported Trump made up the majority of white voters? Did I, deep down, despite everything, even at this late date, consider whites to be the "real" Americans, and is that the reason I was now questioning my relationship to America? Was I, who had always denied being hung up on race, more hung up than I realized?*

My first thought was that Murray would encourage me to listen to some jazz, to take in the lessons of improvisation. But my second thought was that he might suggest the blues instead.

I recall a passage from Murray's book *The Hero and the Blues*:

> [T]he blues statement is nothing if not an experience-confrontation device that enables people to begin by accepting the difficult, disappointing, chaotic, absurd, which is to say the farcical or existential facts of life. Moreover, even as it does so it also prepares or disposes people to accept the necessity for struggle.

Murray might well have said to me: See, you're talking about improvising, like you're trying to find a way around the problem. But you've got to face the problem before you can solve it. The blues is a way of facing what is in front of you.

What were my blues? What did I have to confront there before I could take on the struggle? What form would my struggle take?

In Chapter One I mentioned, so briefly that some may have missed it, that my mother was a widow during my boyhood. My father was fifty-three years old when he had a fatal heart attack. I was eleven at the time. Onto the wet clay of my psyche was imprinted the idea, the fear, the belief that fifty-three years was about what I had to work with, too. When you're young, fifty-three seems an age by which all essential wisdom has been gained, by which one has become the person one is to be. It is possible and desirable to continue learning at fifty-three, of course; but to learn at this stage, surely, is merely to add detail to the great canvas of our conception of life, to color and shade those areas that our experience and wisdom have already sketched in, to see more vividly the picture we know is there — not to toss away the canvas and start all over again.

I was fifty-three years old on the night Donald Trump was elected president. (In one of those coincidences that would start eyes rolling if it appeared in a novel, on the day of Trump's inauguration I had lived *exactly* as long as my father.) At the very age that, consciously or unconsciously, I had always believed I should have everything figured out, I began instead to wonder seriously if I understood anything at all. To my disorientation was added a feeling of shame. *There's no fool like an old fool.* But was I a fool? Perhaps the certainty that I had been a fool might have made things clearer, if no less painful. But: Was it pure, willfully blind stubbornness, and nothing more, to go on championing the concept of the individual when whites as a group had brought us centuries of treatment ranging from unfair to inhuman — and when they had now given us Donald Trump? Or was defending a moral principle most important when no one else on Earth wanted to hear about it? Surely, to have achieved the wisdom I had always associated with the age of fifty-three was to know the answer.

But what I had to confront was that I did not know the answer. For as much as I had learned in my five-plus decades, I might as well have been back in kindergarten, assuming I could fit my ass into one of those little chairs or sit cross-legged on the floor without getting stuck down there.

Knowing nothing, though, has this advantage: everything you see, you see clearly, not through the lens of what you think you know. Maybe this clear sight, if only I could sustain it, would bring me some answers. What I needed to see, and hear, was not to be seen and heard in my apartment or my neighborhood. I had to talk to people I didn't already know. My struggle would be to make sense of what I encountered; the risk would be concluding that the beliefs that had sustained me my whole life were, incontrovertibly, based on nothing.

Three

In my completely unscientific way, to determine where I stood with my countrymen, to decide how I felt about them, to get a feel for just a little of what was going on in this country about which I had developed such uncertain feelings, I wanted to talk to a few people outside my usual circle. I put a post on Facebook announcing that I would like to interview, among others, Trump voters — not skinheads or Ku Kluxers but people who *wouldn't* want to kill me; I did not want to argue with anyone, I informed my Facebook friends, but to listen. Susan Kaufman, a high school friend of my wife's who lives in Los Angeles, told me that she and her husband, Alan, could put me up for as long as I needed and introduce me to one or two people out there. Soon I was in touch with my college friend Donna May — like Susan, a California Democrat — who said that she and her husband could help, too.

On an overcast Friday morning in late May 2017 in Southern California, Susan drove me to a gated community — the first one I'd ever been near — in Moorpark. Stopping the car before a black gate, she phoned her poker pal, whom we will call Bob, for the numbers to punch in on the black box. Code entered, the gates opened slowly, and we drove down the first street on the left to the house, where Bob and his wife, a white couple, let us in. The house made me think of the kind on old-style TV police dramas, with that environment of understated wealth in which the detective would find himself as he arrived to question the friendly-up-to-a-point homeowner about his relationship to the murder victim. The foyer was large, with twin staircases to the left and right curving upward to the second floor; looking up there, I saw many paintings, competent if not exciting landscapes, on the walls. These were the work of Bob's wife — "I just play," she told me — who stood before us now, a slender woman in her late sixties or early seventies, with brownish-blond hair that did not meet her shoulders. And then there was Bob, seventy-two, with a full head of white hair and a pronounced widow's peak, wearing a loose-fitting white T-shirt and tan shorts. His skin, just a little loose around the joints, was very tan, too, with pink flecks. Physically he reminded me of a now-forgotten *Dick Tracy* comic strip villain, Little Face Finney — small features that seemed to get smaller when he winced, as he would at several points in our conversation. After hellos and small talk, Susan and Bob's wife went off together, and Bob and I walked farther into the house, a boundaryless panorama of home where the large kitchen, on the left, blended into the dining area, which blended into the large living room. We sat at the dining table, where I began to record our exchange.

Bob, as he told me, was an only child, born and raised in an entirely white community in Milwaukee. His mother was a homemaker; his father owned a series of taverns when Bob was growing up, and the family lived on the premises, with their quarters separated from the tavern by a door. "I was, I would say, raised poor," he told me. "I had really no interest in school, and as it turned out I didn't do well in school." However, "When I was young I realized the value of money and I started out entrepreneuring as early as I could to make a buck. Dad started out [the day] working in the tavern and I would get up in the mornings and sweep the floors, and you'd be surprised how much money I would find on the weekends, on the Fridays and Saturdays. My biggest find was a five dollar bill in about 1951, which was a lot of money in those days. I mean it's probably equal to $50 today, or more. So that was my first part." When Bob was twelve he got a paper route, and around the same time he struck up an acquaintance with the owner of the sporting goods store across the street, finding and selling the owner nightcrawlers—fishing bait—for a penny apiece. The store sold boats and outboard motors, and after Bob began working there full-time, the owner taught him to repair motors. After he graduated from high school, Bob applied that skill to his work for various car dealerships, where he "made a killing."

There was in Bob's voice, as in the singing of a trio, a blend of elements — humility, pride, wonder; he seemed to marvel all at once at the modesty of his boyhood circumstances, the opportunities that nonetheless presented themselves, and his own success in taking advantage of them. *This is what is possible in America*, he seemed to be saying without using the words. His is an up-by-the-bootstraps narrative, reflecting, he says, an attitude instilled in part by his father. After Bob got his driver's license, for example, his father asked him, "Would you like a car?" "I said sure. Yeah, yeah. I'm all excited. Dad says, 'No problem. You can have a car. You've just got to figure out how you're going to pay for it.'"

Bob bought his own car. "This car cost me $475," he told me, "and had 29,000 miles on it, five years old — to give you an idea how money was. I bought it, paid cash. Long story on the rest of my life, every vehicle I've bought since then I've paid cash. And here's what you do. When you get enough money for the second one you pay cash. While you have the second one you save money for the third one and that's how my life has gone. I've lived that way." If I am to believe him — and I have no reason not to — that approach to money and purchases enabled him to afford, on his salary as a California Highway Patrolman, the house we were sitting in.

He came by that job this way: when he was drafted,

the recruiter asked what he was interested in, and Bob said he had an interest in law enforcement. The recruiter suggested that Bob take tests to see if he qualified for the military police. Bob did well — "the kid who had no interest in school, you know?" — and found himself in military intelligence school in Baltimore. Eventually he was stationed in California. With the end of his military commitment approaching, "I still had my law enforcement in me," so he took more tests. "I'm in Sacramento. I look into the California Highway Patrol, Sacramento County Sheriff, Sacramento Police Department. I take the tests for all three. I missed the Sheriff by one point. I passed the PD and I passed the CHP. I went into CHP. I wanted traffic more than I wanted to do the crime part of it all." He retired in 2000, after thirty-one years.

On the college Scholastic Aptitude Test, so I'm told, you get two hundred points just for signing your name. So let's give Bob some initial credit here: for welcoming me into his home and talking to me openly about his life, for seeming so — what's the word? — *reasonable*. Hell, I'll even say that, listening to his easy, friendly tones, I started to like him a little. That was why, despite my mental preparation, despite my spirit of open-mindedness, despite the fact that I already knew the answer to the question, I was inwardly startled when I asked Bob, "Do you mind telling me who you voted for in the presidential election?" and he replied, in the same friendly, endearing voice I had been hearing all along, "Trump."

Perhaps some will be surprised at my surprise. But consider this variation on an old saying: you can't pick your relatives, but you can pick your friends. With some exceptions, black people do not tend to support Donald Trump, and certainly no one in my family did; unlike many white liberals, I do not find that discussions among extended family become acutely uncomfortable when the subject turns to politics. And while I have white friends, I *choose* those friends, and I do not choose, as a rule, from among conservative Republicans. So while the world of my acquaintances is diverse in some ways, it is bubble-like in others. That is, of course, partly what I was in Bob's house to correct.

Lord help me, I am not a sociologist, and I did not go about these interviews in anything like a scientific way. I simply talked with a handful of people, asking questions *not in search of information but in the hope of understanding*, hoping their ideas might give me some insights into how some of the country thinks. In any case, my conversation with Bob, edited for clarity and relevance, sprinkled with color commentary, went like this:

"What do you feel are his best qualities?" I asked.

"Being Donald Trump," Bob told me. "Everything that that man has done, starting with *The Apprentice* — 'You're fired' — that's where I got to know him. And all the things that he's done —" Bob started to choke up a bit here. "I get emotional over him, because I feel bad he's being — they're being so bad with him — he is doing everything that's right for this country right now. I don't know what he's done that's not right.

"Donald Trump, he's trying to do right by you and me. He's trying to give you a job. He's trying to make sure you have a life, a home, and you have insurance, health insurance and everything. He also wants to make sure that you don't overpay in taxes. He wants to make sure that you can live the American Dream. That's what he's trying to do and unfortunately he is one man and unfortunately he's only got eight years if he gets re-elected, and unfortunately, you look at CNN, no, NBC—93 percent is negative towards Trump. When Barack Obama was in there it was 41 percent negative towards Barack Obama. I like the way Trump talks. You look at people talk. When's the last time," Bob asked, that I saw someone "stand in front of a podium like he has? Has he ever stammered or stuttered a word? Think about that. Never that I've seen. I'm looking for it. I'm waiting for it. He says what he's going to say and he doesn't"—here Bob imitated a stutter, meant, I think, to suggest obfuscation. "He doesn't do that. He comes right out and gives you straight answers. He lacks the experience with government that would make his life easier. But he didn't get into office because he was a politician. We needed an outsider. He is it, and he is going to make a difference. If the press and the Democrats would work with him, we'd all be better off. That's just my opinion."

Was the desire to give me health insurance, I wondered sitting there, behind the attempt to destroy the

Affordable Care Act? Hearing all this might best be compared to listening as a grown man explains his complete faith in Santa Claus. Bob's take on the president seemed to me, to put it as kindly as I can, an instance of seeing what you want to see, and in this context the choice of the words "American Dream" is more appropriate than Bob knows. But we will come back to this in a bit.

"I'm curious about your take on something," I said. "A lot of black and brown people see that groups like the Ku Klux Klan, for example, endorsed Trump, and as far as I know Trump didn't do anything to distance himself from those groups. So when Trump was elected, a lot of black and brown people thought, well, if people voted for this man — if this man got elected who has been endorsed by the Klan, and he didn't distance himself from the Klan, that must mean that the country as a whole is racist. How do you respond to that?"

"Oh, that's hard." Bob seemed pained here, looking down at the table. "I...I just can't see it being that. You have to deal with the circumstances. The Ku Klux Klan or any other organization out there is what it is. And every president, whether you're a woman, a man, black or white or brown or whatever, they're confronted with the same ideologies. And I don't think you — I don't think there's an effect from the Klan. I really don't. I may be wrong on that but... I don't have a real strong good answer for you on that."

"Do you think Trump should have distanced himself

from the Klan?" I asked. "Or do you think he had to do what he had to do to get elected?"

"I think he was trying to do the same for everybody, and I think if you're zeroing in on the Klan—if a lot of people were looking for the reaction from him about the Klan and then that would make him a good guy or a bad guy, he's just a victim of circumstances, I think. Should he have distanced himself? Why would he distance himself from the Ku Klux Klan and not from another group? I might have missed something here with him and the Ku Klux Klan, but is what you're proposing—did it happen?"

"Well, they endorsed him."

"They endorsed him. Well. It doesn't surprise me."

"Mm hmm," I said.

Bob told me at another point in our conversation that he watches a lot of Fox News, which, he said without a trace of irony, is "trying to be fair and balanced." But he had not heard about the KKK endorsement. Go figure. And are you really "just a victim of circumstances" if the dogs hear your whistle and come running? In any case, Bob displayed here a very human tendency—one that is certainly not limited to Trump voters—to look past what you don't want to think about in order to believe what you want, or need, to believe. The question then becomes: What is behind the need to believe it? We will come back to this, too.

"You said a while ago," I continued, "that you feel like lack of civility is a problem today, a lack of civility among people. Does Donald Trump strike you as being uncivil? The way he talks about people? Do you feel like that's a problem that he has, being civil?"

"I don't think he's uncivil. I think he will treat you the same when you're not talking to him. He gets in front and calls it, you know, the fake news, and calls people by names he makes up. To me he is making reference to the whole group, not to you as an individual. It just might be a newscaster and you might be working for CNBC and he may say, 'You're fake news.' The group as a whole might be, but you might be the one guy in here that's not, and he's just using names."

I was working on making sense of that—I'm still working on it—when Bob continued, "And you know what is nice about Trump" (there he used an adjective and a proper noun I had never before heard in the same sentence) "is all these things you're talking about and all these names and shortcomings, he doesn't seem to ever—do you ever see him get upset about anything? Do you ever see him get mad and stomp off or slam down or do anything? He doesn't do any of that."

"Would you," I said, working to keep the incredulity out of my voice, "say the United States is a divided nation? And if so, who's it divided between?"

"Yeah. I say it's divided and it all has to do with Congress. And a division to me is Democrats and Republicans. And until they can go and sit at the Capitol and cross the aisle on every issue, we've got a divided country."

"Do you feel like one side is more to blame than the other for not reaching across the aisle? Or do you feel it's the same on both sides?"

"I think it's pretty hard to get rid of the flu until you take a flu shot. And these people sitting on both sides of the aisle are not getting each other's inoculations, if you will, so a Democrat can see the way the Republicans see and the Republicans can see the way the Democrats see. It goes back to schools, and the colleges they went to, and what they learned at college. That follows them through their life — the neighborhoods they live in, the states they live in, and the jobs that they do, maybe all Democratic — and you're never going to get that person to become a Republican. I don't know how you could."

I would later come across these two excerpts from speeches:

We come from different parties, but we are Americans first. And that's why disagreement cannot mean dysfunction. It can't degenerate into hatred. The American people's hopes and dreams are what matters, not ours. Our obligations are to them. Our regard for them compels us all, Democrats and Republicans, to cooperate, and compromise, and act in the best interests of our nation — one nation, under God, indivisible with liberty and justice for all.
—President Barack Obama, following the end of a government shutdown, October 17, 2013

Our top political priority over the next two years should be to deny President Obama a second term.

—Senate majority leader Mitch McConnell, speaking before the Heritage Foundation, November 4, 2010

"My first encounter with black people was on the Highway Patrol at the Academy. Instructors," Bob told me.

"That's interesting."

"I had a sergeant who was a black person that I really, really liked. And I don't have anything against any color of skin. I don't care what color you are. You are who you are, and I like you for who you are, not what color your skin is. I treated everybody on the road the same way.

" 'The reason why you stopped me is 'cause I'm driving a red Corvette.' The fact that you're going 80 miles an hour in a 65 zone have anything to do with that? 'You stopped me 'cause I'm black!' No, I didn't stop you 'cause you're black, I stopped you because you made a turn from the wrong lane. This is the kind of thing that I dealt with.

"I only have one thing that I've done in my life in law enforcement involving a black person I regret. Should I say what it is?"

"Please."

"I mean it's not nice."

"Please."

"Okay. I'm not going to offend you?"

"I'm not here to judge you."

"Okay. One night I was working the road and I stopped a Los Angeles Lakers center. Tall black guy."

"Chamberlain? Wilt Chamberlain?"

"Wilt Chamberlain," Bob said, nodding. "I stopped Wilt Chamberlain and he's driving a car with Pennsylvania plates. And when I stopped him he was speeding, and he was so big that he didn't sit where you normally sit. His seat was really pushed back, you know. I stopped him—I knew who he was—I can't even tell you today if I wrote him a ticket or not, 'cause it was so long ago.

"And this is the embarrassing part. When we got to the debriefing"—with the other highway patrolmen—"and I'm sitting there and everybody tells war stories. I said, 'I stopped Wilt Chamberlain.' And they said, 'So how did that go?' I says, 'Well, I don't know. He's just a typical nigger.'

"And as it turns out, Joe Collins"—that is not the name Bob told me—"was sitting in the room, and I didn't know him. His back and my back were back to back. He's a black man. And all of a sudden the room went—total silence. And I go, oh shit, I did something. I look around and oh, it was Joe. So I get up, turned around, and I stood up and I apologized to Joe. Not being derogatory—it just came out, if you will, and I didn't mean anything by it, but that is one of the things that I regret.

"To this day on the Highway Patrol, that's the only thing I've ever said that really hurt me. And I'm telling you now, thirty-five to forty years later, that's what it was. But the N word is not used today like it used to be. In that day, everybody said it. We're going back into the early seventies."

"When you said it," I asked, "what do you think you meant by it?"

"What I think I meant—he was just slow and lethargic to what I was selling. He was in a different world, and he didn't interact with my world. And he thought he was different than me, either better or worse or whatever. It wasn't a good interaction if you will, and I've caught that dealing with other black people. Never ever good. They—they almost had a different gait to them, different words to them."

"A different gait? You mean a different walk?"

"Oh, a different walk." At this point, I am guessing, Bob forgot whom he was talking to. "They just—you know, they just ho-hummed around and walk differently. Not everybody, but I mean they just were different. And that's just the way they are, and that's okay and they talk and they have all their jibber jabber jive and stuff that they talk and I go, 'Whatever.'"

I have to say, first, with absolute sincerity—and you can scream "Uncle Tom" at me all you want—that I admire Bob for telling me the story about Wilt Chamberlain. He did not have to do it, and, as he surely knew, the story does not flatter him. What he did not know, I'm guessing, is the extent to which he contradicted himself in a very short time, making the light-year trip from "I don't have anything against any color of skin. I don't care what color you are" to "never ever good/jibber jabber jive." It would, of course, be — pick your adjective: pointless, dishonest, disingenuous — to claim that there are not cultural differences between many black Americans and many white Americans, and Bob, in his way, acknowledged that. But difference, once acknowledged, should be accepted without disparagement, and this is where my friend Bob fell short, "never ever good" and "jibber jabber jive" suggesting an attitude a couple of notches down from respect. How can one head hold both "I don't care what color you are" and "jibber jabber jive"? It helps enormously if the owner of said head is blind to the negativity of his own attitudes, which could possibly explain a great deal, about Bob and a whole lot of other people. Police officers. Hiring managers. Elementary school teachers.

"So," I said, "you said your first exposure to black people was in your line of work. So there were some people you worked with, and some black people you encountered on the road. When you encountered black people on the road, did you — after a while, when you saw a black person that you stopped, do you feel like you developed a way of thinking about them before you interacted with them?"

"I told you this earlier and I'll stand with it," Bob told me. "I treated everybody the same."

"Do you think there's a level playing field in the US?" I wanted to know. "Do people of all different groups have more or less the same chances for success?"

"No," Bob said. "It has to do with where you're living and it has to do with who your parents are. You're a product of your environment, and your environment starts with your grandparents, great grandparents, great grandparents' parents. You are a victim of your circumstances and the environment in which you were born and raised. It's where you are, when. The first eighteen years of your life is when you are being programmed by your parents and whatever your parents do. Not everybody has a chance. I haven't spent a whole lot of time down in LA. There is the inner city and those poor kids down there—and I've driven down there a few times and—they don't have a prayer in hell to be successful and get a chance to go to college and graduate and get a job. What do they learn how to do? They learn that the only way they can make ends meet is they become a product of their environment, and a lot of it is gangs. They learn how to become a part of a gang and then they wind up going the wrong way."

"You were talking about kids in the inner city and how they don't have a chance," I said. "When you think of the problems that exist in the inner city, how much of the problems there are imposed from without, and how much are the fault of the people in the inner city?"

"I think all of us fault the people in the inner city because they are the product of the environment that they were raised in. They're all raised in the inner city so they don't know any different. They don't have an opportunity to get out.... Let's say we had a family and the father dies and the mother is alive but she can't handle the kids or something and you take them and put them into adoption. Those kids, probably the best thing that ever happened to them is getting away from their mom and dad and the inner city and going someplace else, and live with even black people outside of the inner city. Put them with white people outside the inner city and they will become a better person for themselves and for our country. It's unfortunate that that's the way it is. I think it all goes back to the beginning when the people first came to this country and the black people were slaves and then they became—they got their independence and became citizens. But it started that way and it's still there."

Okay, well...if I have to explain the issues with "even black people outside of the inner city" and "Put them with white people outside the inner city and they will become a better person for themselves and for our country," there really may be no hope. But every so often, when putting on an old record, you hear a note or two you missed before. Let's see:

The problems inherent in viewing oneself as representing the norm and others as deviating from that norm may be obvious, but what may be less obvious is how common such viewing is. A white woman I know, who voted for Obama twice, who would be horrified at an accusation of prejudice, once asked me about my hair, "If you combed it out, would it be straight?" The assumption behind that question — *I am the norm, you are the deviation* — is the very one at the heart of the suggestion that black inner-city children would be better off with whites, those representatives of normal humanity, than with their own families. Lest anyone is tempted to defend himself by defending Bob, to explain away Bob's view by stressing the importance of culture over that of skin color, let us ponder the phrase "*even* black people outside of the inner city" (emphasis mine). Presumably, black people outside the inner city have separated themselves from inner-city culture (which is assumed to be evil, an assumption we'll let go for the moment) — but the remaining problem seems to be that, dammit, *they're still black*. Nonetheless, *even black people* outside the inner city would do a better job with those kids than would the kids' families in the inner city. Blacks outside it, after all, probably enjoy the normalizing influence of whites.

That attitude, at its most malignant, brings about the separation of family members, a topic we will return to. Viewing oneself as a representative of the norm can make for the worst, most harmful and irreparable acts of racism, but it can also give one, in one's own mind, the power of magnanimity. What makes a person feel better about himself than magnanimity? What is more magnanimous than accepting others *despite their deviation from the norm you represent*? And granting such acceptance gives one a kind of line of moral credit. Maybe, for example, you voted for that nice young black fella; maybe you even did it twice. That entitles you to think about *yourself* for once, right? Maybe let's give Trump a chance, after all that magnanimity. And who is more magnanimous than a liberal? The words even have similar meanings. (Amy once asked me, "Do you ever feel like your white male friends really like you, but your being black just gives things that extra *umph* for them?")

But any finger I point is ultimately directed at myself, too. In the course of my teaching, I have had a small handful of transgender students. If I have treated those students any differently from the way I've treated others, I am not aware of it, and certainly no one has complained about me in that regard. I take a silent pride, in fact, in how easy and normal my relations with transgender students have been, and it is that pride that damns my soul, based as it is in an assumption of fundamental difference, of a position from which to be magnanimous — a magnanimity that can be withdrawn as well as given. One can't help one's feelings, and I don't know if it is possible for a person of my generation to feel differently. But of course those are excuses. In a society where "majority" is synonymous with "normal," justice will remain elusive. While we're convicting Bob, we might think about consulting a lawyer ourselves.

"So," I said to Bob, "you think that what's happening in the inner city is a legacy from slavery?"

"I think it's the aftermath of it. It's the continuation of it only through the generations. It's just continued on."

"Do you think what's happening in the inner city is at all because of ongoing discrimination?"

Bob paused a while here. "Hmm. I would like to say no to that question. But I don't think I can say that 100 percent."

"Okay."

"Ah, I think there is some of that there. I really do."

To put that answer—reasonable and even generous on its face—in perspective: imagine that a person is asked if the world may be round. Imagine that the person answers: "I think there is something to that theory. I really do." Such an answer would suggest a lack of knowledge of basic facts about the world. Similarly, in a country where racial discrimination and discrepancies have been documented everywhere from the classroom to the employment office to the ballot box to the courtroom, to say "I think there is some" racial discrimination is to admit to a profound lack of knowledge. That lack is certainly not the only factor explaining Donald Trump's election, but it is a big one. And even knowledge brings its own ignorance. How would a figure such as Donald Trump appear to someone who is uncertain about the existence of racism in America? Here is where *I* lack knowledge. I honestly don't know.

I can guess, though. You see that black and brown people together make up 29 percent of the US population and 59 percent of the prison population. Take away the explanation involving a racist criminal justice system, and what conclusion are you left with? For someone arriving at the logical conclusion via incomplete knowledge, Trump might seem blunt on the subject of race, with his talk of "bad hombres" and his crazily inaccurate claim that blacks kill 81 percent of white homicide victims — blunt, but not wrong or racist. The *generous* explanation in that case (and, in fact, the one that Bob supplied) is that black and brown people have messed-up families.

But just as I was about to cut Bob some slack, he dropped this on me: "There's a little difference between the Spanish people and the black people and I don't know what it is, and I told you that earlier. They are different and I don't know why it is."

"How are they different?"

"I think the Spanish people want to be successful more than the black people do. They've come here. They got themselves across the border. They paid their way to get here, fought their way to get here. They fight their way to stay here. The black people that are here legally and are born here legally — but they're just in the wrong mindset to do better."

Oh, Bob. Of course, the most exasperating person in the world is the one who reminds you of yourself. What was that I wrote earlier? *I wondered if black people should be doing something to help ourselves, something central and crucial, something that had little to do with white racism, that we weren't doing.*

Oh, Clifford.

"Let me ask you this," I said to Bob. "The reports about unarmed black people being shot by police — when you hear about that, what do you think has happened?"

"I wonder why it happens. Okay? I've carried a gun half my life and I know that I can use it and I've been taught to use it. I don't shoot to hurt you. I'm shooting to kill you. That's how we're taught. Shoot to kill. Double tap, two shots, center mass. But when you shoot you better be justified in your shooting."

"What about when the black person is unarmed?" I said. "What do you think happens in those situations?"

"That's what we're getting to. I may have no reason to shoot you. [But] if the dispatcher says, 'You've got Cliff Thompson on Watson Drive. He's driving whatever kind of car and he's armed and dangerous' — Well, lights go on now. And now I get you and I've been told you're armed and dangerous. Some of these officers out there — not everybody's trained as well as I was, okay? And there are police officers that have a hard time with the English language out there in small communities. There's nobody there. Not very educated, got a high school education, doesn't talk well, doesn't understand well. And gets into a situation where he may overreact to certain circumstances. The cop probably wants to be safe rather than sorry, and he'd rather it be you than him. But once you find out the circumstances and you kill a fifteen-and-a-half-year-old kid that doesn't have a gun…that wouldn't play well personally for me for the rest of my life. I'm having a hard time calling Wilt Chamberlain an N word, you know. And that bothers me."

"I don't know if this is a different question or the same question again," I said to Bob, "but what do you think explains the fact, or the perception, that there's a disproportionate number of unarmed black people who are shot? What do you think explains that?"

"Okay. I don't have the question clear to me," Bob said.

"It would seem that the number of unarmed black people who are shot is disproportionate to the numbers of black people in the population."

"Give me an example of what you're talking about here."

"Well. Let's say—I don't know if these figures are exactly right."

"Doesn't have to be." (As it turned out, they were very close.)

"Okay. So let's say black people make up 12 percent of the US population."

"Okay."

"But let's say they make up 25 or 30 percent of the people who are unarmed and get killed. What do you think explains that?"

Bob looked positively anguished here. "There—" he chuckled, mirthlessly. "I would say that the dispropor-tionate thing is that, when you take the number of peo-ple that are black, the number that are black that are committing crimes is higher in percentage than their percentage is.

"They are putting themselves in harm's way doing the things they do. It's not a question of if; it's going to hap-pen. And you just don't want it to be you. And how does that not become you? You change your life and you go to school, get educated and get a job and never have to deal with a gang, crimes and all the things that they go through."

"So if you're black and you're unarmed and you get shot and killed," I said, "and you haven't done anything, do you think that that person is paying the price for what somebody else has done?"

"I wouldn't be surprised. I wouldn't be surprised."

"Do you think that the officer who does it is perhaps thinking of this other guy, this criminal he has in his mind…And the person he shoots is paying the price for that?"

"I think that if that officer's been in that precinct and working that beat long enough, what you're saying has truth to it. I think if he's coming on that beat the first time, ain't gonna happen. But if multiple times, the more exposure he has…When you start dealing with people that have no respect for law enforcement, have no respect for their own lives and are willing to say or do anything 'cause they've got nothing to lose, they're going to become a victim of circumstances and that's going to be the thought process of the guy that you're talking about."

*　*　*

My college friend Donna May and her husband, George Flores, live on a street in Toluca Lake, California, with one-story houses and several distinct kinds of trees, including tall palms. At the end of the street is Jack's house. ("Jack" is not his real name.) Donna walked me down there. A black vintage car that looked to be from the 1920s—which I would ride in later—sat in front of it. A white picket fence and tall bushes surround the modest-sized house and small yard. Jack answered the door and with a friendly manner asked us inside. He is a white man, fairly large, completely bald, with a full, Santa Claus–like white beard; he wore a gray Air Force T-Shirt, jeans, and sneakers. As Donna departed, Jack led me through the house—a little cluttered, with low ceilings—and into the small backyard. Jack's two dogs, both curly-haired, one white and one gray, pawed me the whole time. In the backyard we sat at a table, and Jack produced two bottles of beer. I thanked Jack for having me over, we clinked bottles, and I began to record our conversation.

Jack, he told me, is a third-generation native Californian, seventy-two years old, like Bob. He grew up in Northern California, about eighty miles east of San Francisco; his father was a grain farmer. "My dad and all the other farmers were, you know, pretty much old white guys," he said. His parents were both "diehard Democrats." As a boy Jack worked on the farm, "enough to know that it was something I didn't want to do." He graduated from Stanford University in 1966, at a time when "it was either you joined" the military "or you got drafted," so he joined the Air Force and flew 237 combat missions in Vietnam. "You can't describe it to somebody who hasn't done it," he told me. Photography had been a hobby of Jack's; he gradually moved from still photography to film, so after his discharge he spent two years in film school in Santa Barbara. From there he made his way into advertising, working for a firm I had heard of and spending forty-five years making TV commercials before retiring.

I asked Jack if he was a liberal, like his parents, as a young man.

"Yeah. I was liberal. The first presidential election I would have voted in, I think, it was — I voted for McGovern, God help me. Which in hindsight was just idiotic. But when I got out of the service I didn't think too much about politics — other than I really hated the politicians who wouldn't let us finish the job over there, but that's another story for another book. But I remember I spent a couple of weeks of that summer at a friend's house up in Lake Tahoe, a rental they had up there — and my friend's mother was very, very conservative. And — actually this was kind of a turning point for me.

"We were sitting around one night having some drinks and I'm going on about McGovern this, McGovern that, and she sits down across from me where you are and says, 'Jack, now I know you're a smart guy. You know, you went to Stanford with my son and blah blah blah blah blah. So tell me what it is — and I really want to know — why is it that you prefer George McGovern? Is it his policies?' And I didn't have an answer.

"It was just that I fancied myself as a Democrat, and he was a Democrat, and that's what it was — and I didn't like Nixon. But his policies? Hell, I probably didn't know what his policies were. And then all of a sudden it dawned on me: you know, I need to be smarter than this. I need to at least know where people are coming from and what they're doing. And I think there's not a whole lot of that even today. I mean people just kind of blindly go one way or another."

"Would you have described yourself more as a conservative after that moment?"

"Yeah, I sort of started tilting a little bit that way. And then, you know, as you get out into the workaday world and you start making a little bit of money, conservatism sort of makes more sense."

"So you witnessed the civil rights movement, the women's movement," I said.

"Yeah. Yeah."

"Do you remember what your opinions were at the time of those movements and of the sixties in general?"

"I don't think I quite understood enough about it. I knew there was all this upheaval and these movements and stuff. The civil rights movement wasn't really big on my radar because it didn't really involve me. At least I didn't think it did. In the sixties of course the war was the big thing. And then there was something else you mentioned, civil rights and…"

"The women's movement."

"The women's movement, yeah. That more or less came, I think, in the seventies. I remember I was in film school, and we were out having drinks, and there's a young woman with us—I didn't know her and she was a guest of somebody else—and she was very…I don't know if 'militant' would be the right word, but she was very much a feminist.

"And she started talking about the inequity in the workplace that women experience. I remember telling her, 'Let's take your point that men have an unfair advantage over women in the workplace and let's agree to that. Now why would I, as a man, want to change that?' That didn't make her very pleased. So.

"But I don't know. I always kind of looked at the women's movement kind of—not that I was amused by it, but it was…Well, once again, I'm not black and I'm not a woman, so maybe I should be more aware of these things but I don't know."

"So you said a minute ago that when you get out into the workaday world, conservatism makes more sense to you. Can you explain that to me?"

"I think fiscal conservatism is holding on to your money, is lower taxes, is keeping more of your money, having the government take less of it. Not to say that all Republicans have done that. God help us. But at least that's the philosophy. I think it just makes more sense, at least to me."

"Can you tell me — what do you think is good about life in the United States?"

"Freedom is the quick answer. I mean, you can do anything you want. You can be anything you want. If you work hard you can be successful. I mean all those clichés — but they're true."

"What do you see as the main problems facing the country?"

"Oh Jesus, where to start. Um…" He sighed heavily. "Well, the main problems right now are, in no particular order, terrorism — and it's going to get bigger and bigger I'm afraid. The political divide — that the two sides simply will not talk to each other. It's a little frightening, and it's going to take somebody that we don't even know who it is yet to bring those sides together I think, so there's that, the big political divide."

Let's look for a minute at that "big political divide." In March 2016, in the last year of his presidency, Barack

Obama nominated Merrick Garland for a seat on the US Supreme Court. Garland has been called a centrist and is, in any case, no flaming liberal, and Obama's decision to nominate him can be seen as a preemptive compromise with congressional Republicans, made in the hope of getting a nominee approved. It is tempting to say that Obama miscalculated, except that that term does not apply to a situation in which success is simply not possible. The Republican-controlled Senate, in an unprecedented move, refused to vote on the nomination, ostensibly because Obama was a lame-duck president and as such, according to logic I confess is beyond me, did not represent the will of the American people — never mind that Obama, lame duck or not, was seeking to fulfill one of the most important duties the American people had elected him to perform. Senate majority leader Mitch McConnell said, "The American people are perfectly capable of having their say on this issue, so let's give them a voice. Let's let the American people decide. The Senate will appropriately revisit the matter when it considers the qualifications of the nominee the next president nominates, whoever that might be." We all know who that next president turned out to be: a man who received less than half of the popular vote and yet got his Supreme Court nominee approved. So much for letting the American people decide.

This was not a case of "the two sides simply not talking to each other"; this was a case of one side talking and the other covering its ears and saying, "La la la, not listening." Why assign equal blame in a situation in which one side is so clearly in the wrong?

That is one question. I posed another question earlier: "Bob displayed here a very human tendency—one that is certainly not limited to Trump voters—to look past what you don't want to think about in order to believe what you want, or need, to believe. The question then becomes: What is behind the need to believe it?" I believe the two questions have the same answer.

And that answer comes back, once again, to the concept of rootedness. What both Bob and Jack are rooted in, it seems to me, is the belief that America is essentially a land of freedom and fairness. Bob's self-concept, in particular, is rooted in the notion—let's call it the American Dream—that in America you get out of life what you put into it, period. If people have problems in a land where the principles of freedom and fairness prevail, then those problems surely reflect on the people themselves; if it is a given that the system is not flawed, that this essentially fair and free system would simply not allow itself to be hijacked by one political party, that the system is somehow immune to the prejudices of its representatives, then it can be very difficult to locate fault where it otherwise obviously lies. If one refuses to believe that, here in America, a malevolent force is capable of upsetting the ideal, that the basic goodness of the system is ever in danger, then when something is really wrong—say, the suffering in black communities—the fault must lie chiefly with the people doing the suffering. To think otherwise would be to doubt the truth of the ideas in which one is rooted. Such thinking must be avoided at all costs. It would mean waking up from the American Dream.

Rootedness, such a basic human necessity, can have a distorting effect on what one sees. Certainly many— Bob is a fine example—are rooted in the concept of their own normality. But as with other phenomena, the vision-distorting effect of rootedness is not limited to Trump voters. One day when my daughters were small, our little interracial family took a trip by subway. When we got onto the crowded car, a black woman who was seated looked at us, then looked at me, and literally shook with anger, her face a mask of indignation. She had the appearance of someone who had been betrayed in the most personal and therefore hurtful of ways, and, without knowing the woman, I am guessing that that is how she felt. She was obviously reacting to having seen a black man raising a family with a white woman, which she saw as an insult to black people and especially black women—because it is with those people that her identity is rooted. By failing to subscribe to a black identity *as she defined it*, I offended her sense of rootedness. She was angered by what she saw on the subway—which, however, was not *us*, but what was in her own head.

Some appear to find rootedness in the belief—one that I come to understand better every day, even though I stop short of embracing it—that an ongoing plot against black people encompasses any experiences we are likely to have and, without question, explains the bad ones. This belief is itself rooted, it seems to me, in the idea that, given our history, the very worst thing a black person can do is to allow himself to be fooled—that it is therefore better to be suspicious of everything than to be taken in by anything.

But back to Jack on the problems facing the nation:

"The national debt is terrifying. Twenty trillion dollars? That's what? That's a time bomb tickin'. You know racism seems to have reared its ugly head a little bit more lately." (Did he toss that one in for my benefit?)

"So you said the political divide," I said. "Do you think that's the main divide in the country, between Democrats and Republicans in Congress? Or where do you see fault lines in the country?"

"Well, just politics, Left versus Right. I see economics, haves versus have-nots. I guess that's probably the crux of it. To my point of view, the Democrats are trying to buy votes by giving shit away and have been fairly successful at doing that. I mean hell. The open border on the southern border was nothing more than a Democratic voter drive as far as I can see.

"And it's funny now. I mean, Trump's new budget's come out this week, or will come out, and people are just railing against the cuts in social services and research and all these different things. And I can understand why that would be upsetting. On the other hand, the government can't take care of everybody. It's not their job to take care of everybody. So there's tough choices."

"So when I asked you what was good about living in the United States, you said freedom off the bat, and if you work hard here that you can succeed."

"Yeah."

"Do you feel there's a more or less equal playing field in the United States? Does everybody have the same chance to succeed?"

"No," Jack said. "I mean my family wasn't rich by any means, but we did okay. But my family had enough money to send me to a good school. There's a whole strata of people out there you know — and mostly young black people who do not have the same opportunities just because they can't afford 'em. There's a lot of young black kids out there without fathers and father figures and parents who are supportive of them. And I don't know how you deal with that. I don't know how you fix it." (*I don't know, either. Maybe some of those social services that got cut as a result of tough choices?*) Jack, whose background is pretty different from Bob's, then said something very similar to what Bob had said: "With young African American kids, I think a lot of it is lack of family structure. I really do. You know, people to look up to and role models and stuff like that."

"To what extent do you think the problems are imposed from without?" I asked. "In other words, to what extent are they the result of ongoing discrimination and to what extent are they just kind of their own troubles?"

"I think they arose out of discrimination. I don't live in that world — I don't see that much discrimination, but I think it's there if you want to see it." His mind made an interesting leap here: "I think that this whole Black Lives Matter movement is total bullshit."

"Why is that?"

"Because — well for example the kid in Illinois — tell me what the name of the town, um... Ferguson."

"Ferguson. Missouri."

"Ferguson, Missouri. Illinois, Missouri. It's all the same place. Anyway, I mean he" — Michael Brown — "was out there — he was doing bad shit, bad stuff, and he got caught, and the cops reacted probably in the right way, and yet it all got twisted completely around about how it was police brutality and it was discrimination blah blah blah blah blah. And it was 'Hands up, don't shoot.' That never happened. The facts get twisted. Politicians are doing the same damn thing, you know. It's one thing and all of a sudden it's not one thing, it's the other thing. And enough people are willing to believe it."

I said, "Are you familiar with the Eric Garner case?"

"Name's familiar. What...?"

"Eric Garner was in New York and he was selling loose cigarettes..."

"Yeah."

"And cops came to get him and — "

"It's comin' to me."

"And they choked him to death, and he said, 'I can't breathe.' They put him in a choke hold, and he said 'I can't breathe.' But they kept the choke hold and he died."

"Right."

"I mean, every case is different, but when you hear about a case like that, what do you think?"

"You know, it doesn't surprise me, because there are bad cops out there who are, I think, in that game because of the power they get. And I don't know that there's a big percentage of them, but they're there and they can sure make it bad for everybody else. I mean you see it all the time. You see videos, especially now everybody's with their phones filming everything. I mean they get people down and they kick 'em and they choke 'em and all this sort of stuff."

Let's stop a moment and consider this. One black man, Eric Garner, dies at the hands of police in what seems a straightforward case of brutality. Another, Michael Brown, dies at the hands of police under circumstances that turn out to have been partially misreported. Jack expressed disapproval of both courses of events, but he had to be reminded of the one involving Eric Garner, perhaps because it was simply part of the natural if regrettable order of things. (I think of what I heard in the cop's laughter: *This is just how it is*.) But the Michael Brown episode got under Jack's skin, representing as it did an unfair indictment of the system in which Jack is rooted, this land of freedom.

"So you voted for Donald Trump," I said to Jack.

"I did."

"What do you see as his best qualities?"

"I think he's a smart businessman and he's going to tackle problems differently than a career politician, and it's going to work sometimes and it's not going to work sometimes. You know, he shoots from the hip a lot. I don't know. It's different. It's gonna be different. We'll see how it works. I hope it works."

"Did you have any reservations about voting for him?"

"Yeah. Well, I mean, like I said, he shoots from the hip you know, and all this — all this, like, juvenile tweeting and stuff that he does. But that's who he is. So we'll see."

"Yeah. So far, is he kind of doing what you expected?"

"Yeah, pretty much. I like that he talks tough about terrorism and I think, given the right set of circumstances, will do something about it, which is totally different than what Obama did, who didn't even give lip service to it. I mean he wouldn't even call it what it was. So I like that. I think his business sense is going to do the country well. I think they are going to end up cutting taxes. You know I don't give a shit — I mean I'm not rich, but I don't give a shit about cutting taxes on the rich and on corporations if it's going to put more money out into the economy. You know, I mean, the Republicans have tried that. They've tried that before. It's worked a little, it hasn't worked a little. But…What else is there? Foreign policy, I think, already has improved. I think we're getting a little more respect around the world than we did, because we couldn't have gotten much less."

"Mm," I said. That might not be the first conclusion one would draw from, for example, this headline in a June 26, 2017, article published on the Web site of the Pew Research Center: "U.S. Image Suffers as Publics Around World Question Trump's Leadership."

"So to backtrack a little bit," I said. "Trump…Well, I'll just say, a lot of black and brown people in the country see that groups like the Ku Klux Klan endorse Trump."

"Yeah. Yeah."

"And he, as far as I know, did not distance himself from that."

"Right."

"So in the view of a lot of black and brown people, if this man gets elected it says about the country that the electorate tolerates racism and is arguably racist itself for having done this."

"Mm hmm."

"So how would you respond to that?"

"I can understand that point of view completely. And what Trump is gonna have to do, and the Republicans are going to have to do, is they're gonna have to start making things better for people and try to disprove that. You know?"

"Do you think he should have distanced himself from that endorsement?"

"Oh absolutely. Why wouldn't you? I mean there's a lot things I think he should or shouldn't have done. Why would you say some of the things he does and tweet some of the things he does? I don't understand it, but I don't know what goes on in his head. But…the Ku Klux Klan comes out and endorses you, you back away from that one. Take two giant steps. Maybe three." (I asked him later, via email, how he justified voting for Trump under these circumstances. He wrote back: "It all boils down to the lesser of two evils. Many of us did not vote for him with any degree of enthusiasm but rather to avoid the horrific prospect of Hillary Clinton in the White House. Had she won the Supreme Court would have had a Far Left majority for the next 2–3 generations, maybe longer and that was the big prize in the last election. I have to believe that most Clinton voters cast their ballots for her with total disregard of her lengthy resume of dishonesty, too lengthy and probably unnecessary to itemize here.")

"So it sounds like maybe Trump is not your ideal president — you might change some things?"

"Well, I mean, no, he's not an ideal president. What the country needs is somebody to unite us, and that's not Trump, and it wasn't Hillary Clinton, and it sure as hell wasn't Bernie Sanders."

"So it wasn't Barack Obama," I said, girding myself.

"It's definitely not a Barack Obama."

"Okay. How would you characterize Obama's presidency?"

"Oh, I thought it was awful. I mean from foreign affairs, which just was disastrous, in every...I mean our standing in the world just plummeted. He would draw the red line in Syria. Well there's no red line in Syria. It's just everything he seemed to touch just didn't turn out. Foreign affairs, the economy certainly did not improve." (*That's not what I've read.*) "I think racism got worse."

"Hmm. Do you think he was responsible for that?"

"A little bit."

"How so?"

"Well the thing in Massachusetts with the cops, and it became a teachable moment." He was referring here to the incident in which the prominent African American scholar Henry Louis Gates was arrested by a white police officer after trying to enter his own house. Gates and the officer later joined Obama in the White House for a "beer summit." "But immediately when the issue came out [Obama] condemned the cops without really knowing what the facts were. So I think he was a little too quick on the trigger to go that way. I just didn't see anything good that he did, and that includes Obamacare.

"It's funny. I play tennis every Saturday morning and almost all the guys I play with are hard Left guys. We just don't talk politics much, and we joke about it from time to time. But I remember, it was a couple of years ago, and I tried this just as a little test. It was at the height of the

IRS goings-on, and Lois Lerner was up to her eyeballs in it, and I asked all these guys I play tennis with, including about maybe twenty other people that I worked with, I said, 'Does the name Lois Lerner mean anything to you?'"

If Jack interpreted my silence here — correctly — as ignorance, he didn't press me on it. I looked up Lerner the minute I got back to Donna's house; she was at the center of a controversy in which the IRS was accused of denying tax-exempt status to conservative organizations. Apparently Jack's tennis pals didn't know who Lerner was, either, because Jack said to me, "I told these guys, I said, 'Well then I hope you don't vote.'" He laughed. "You know? Because — of course I asked the same thing of my wife. My wife had no idea who she was. One or two guys knew, but it was kind of funny." (Jack's wife, he told me, is Hispanic. She does not share his political views.)

"Well," I said. "Can I change tack for a second?"

"Sure."

"We talked a little bit about whether or not there's an equal playing field, and, you know, what's happening with African American kids. How do you come down on affirmative action? What do you think of that?"

"Mm. I think it was a good idea once. I'm not sure it is anymore."

"Why is that?"

"I think we probably moved — I personally kind of think we've moved out of the arena where segregation and racism have that much of an impact where they need to be addressed by affirmative action. It's had its time and it's had its place and I think it was effective. I don't know that we need it now."

"Let me set up a hypothetical situation," I said. "If a black kid grows up *not* in the inner city, not in a poor neighborhood but in a middle-class neighborhood, do you feel that affirmative action should apply to that individual in the college-selection process, and the employment process, or in any way at all?"

"No, I don't. You know — what I think is: we ought to be colorblind. Whether it's black, Hispanic, Asian, white, we ought to be colorblind. I mean I know we're not — but someday."

The thing about color-blindness? It is, as its name suggests, a form of blindness. To refuse to see a person's color is to refuse to see what she may be experiencing because of it. I hasten to point out that judging a person as an individual is not synonymous with being color-blind. To see a person as an individual is to take into account everything about that person. Color-blindness, on the other hand, is the equivalent of not seeing that a person standing up on the subway is pregnant — and, therefore, not even considering offering your seat.

* * *

The part of my conversation with Jack that is relevant to this book pretty much ended there. As I was leaving, I mentioned the black vintage car parked in front of Jack's house; it was not, as I had guessed, a Model T, but a Model A, from 1927, which he had restored. Jack offered to give me a ride back to Donna's house. Since Donna lives just down the street, he took me around the block, giving me a chance to take in the feel of that two-seater, with its loud engine, bare metal floor, and horn that sounds exactly like you think: *ah-OOO-gah*. I felt about my ride in this car the way I imagine some will come to feel about the Trump presidency: it was so shockingly out of date as to be novel, it was fun for a short ride, but not comfortable, or even endurable, over the long haul. We arrived in front of Donna's house, where I shook Jack's hand and got out.

* * *

A Trump voter I'll call Fred was eighty-four years old when I talked with him by phone in June 2017. Fred was born and raised in St. Paul, Minnesota, and now lives in Missouri; he spent decades working for various grain companies there. I first came into contact with Fred through his daughter. She sent me an email through my Web site, asking if I was related to a black man named Clifford Thompson who served in the Korean War; Fred, who is white, had served with him and wanted to find him. Fred himself told me in an email about serving with this other Clifford Thompson: "We were in a unit that consisted of tracked landing vehicles which had

75mm pack howitzers. We dug a long trench and drove the machines into it so we could fire across the Han River at the North Korean troops on the other side. We also dug bunkers behind the vehicles to live in. One evening I was laying on my bunk when we heard dirt falling. Cliff Thompson quickly reached down and grabbed me and jerked me out of the way of the collapsing dirt wall! Cliff always looked out for me and felt I needed to be protected. I guess I did!!"

During my short conversation with Fred, he called Donald Trump "a man who had the backbone to stand up for what he thought, and would say so" (though he did say, when asked if he had any reservations about voting for Trump, that he "found him to be a little impulsive"). Fred also offered his opinion that "the number-one problem we need to face is that terrorism is not going to go away unless we deal with it." Asked about the Ku Klux Klan's endorsement of Trump, Fred said, "I'm not so sure that the endorsement is actually an endorsement. A lot of what I see now in the media I have questions about its reliability. We have a couple of news leaks reporting, I think, on Russia. You'd like to think that the reporting you get from the media is the truth and only that. That seems to be far from the way they work. Companies running an afternoon or an evening news show need to have something spectacular to keep people coming back, and that seems to be what drives the media." Asked about Trump's quote about fondling women, Fred said,

"People love to talk about sex scandals and all the rest of that crap but I don't usually pay an awful lot of attention to it"—which also applied, he said, to the Bill Clinton/ Monica Lewinsky sex scandal.

"Historically," I said to Fred, "African Americans, Latinos, women have been denied certain opportunities on the basis of race and sex and ethnicity. Do you feel that's still the case, or do you feel that the playing field is level across race and gender?"

He replied, "I don't know that the playing field will ever be level. There's a lot more women in industry than a few years ago, and in politics, and running major companies. Now a lot of major corporations today have black CEOs." But, he added, if you'd rather "bang your drum"— i.e., protest in the streets over inequality—than work hard, "you're not going to get very far."

When I asked him what he thought was responsible for conditions in what he referred to as "the ghetto," he said, "That's not a question I can answer. I've never lived in one. You're better off talking to someone who has lived there." He also said, "White or black or brown has never been an issue with me."

*   *   *

Those were my successfully conducted interviews with Trump supporters. My friend Susan, who set up the interview with Bob, also tried to set up one with a police captain in Los Angeles who is a Trump supporter. That individual refused to sit for an interview with me, because of my written description of what I was after, which I include here in part:

> I'm working on a nonfiction book that is a kind of personal tribute to the writer Joan Didion, who is in her 80s now. In her essays, Didion has shown a talent for looking at things as they are, instead of repeating things she's heard and read or looking for evidence of what she already thinks.
>
> My idea is that the country needs that approach very badly right now, and it's an approach I'm trying to take. With Donald Trump's election, and with the rash of shootings of unarmed African Americans by police, among other events, my overall questions are: What is happening in America right now? How do Americans feel about each other, particularly about Americans different from themselves?

The captain told Susan, as she wrote to me, that "the statistics show that there is not a rash of killings of unarmed black people, but Democrats don't believe it even when shown the numbers." I guess he thought I wouldn't believe it, either, so he saw no point in talking to me. Not having learned my lesson, I sent more or less the same description of my project to another Trump voter I had been put in touch with, who seemed willing to be interviewed until he read what I had written. I will call this individual Peter, since, actually, that was his name. Our email exchange went this way:

Clifford,

The juxtaposition of those two premises demonstrate in my mind a less than serious attempt [at] openness and interest in understanding. You could have just as easily attempted to postulate the increase in fires [in] black churches in the South oh wait there hasn't been an increase in that either.

What you have seen is an increase in the capture on video of highly questionable police actions...but the simple placing [of] those two premises side by side demonstrates bias.

Peter

Dear Peter,

I was not attempting to imply a causal link between Trump's election and killings of unarmed blacks. I do have biases, as everyone does, and as I have admitted. I am, however, making a serious attempt at understanding what's going on. I just flew to California (I live in New York) and spent several hours asking questions of, and listening to, two men who voted for Trump. Mainly, I listened. I was hoping for the opportunity to listen to what you have to say, too. Well, thank you for responding to my text and email messages.

Cliff

[from Peter:] If you are not implying a link then you are communicating in nonsequitors? What did you think the only people who voted for Trump were individuals who drive around in oversized pickups and wore stupid hats or a hand full who were attempting to manipulate the public?

I started to respond to that email, then realized there would be no point.

* * *

One thing Jack said — "The government can't take care of everybody. It's not their job to take care of everybody" — reminded me of something.

Not long ago a friend emailed me a link to a trailer for a documentary in which she had been interviewed. Many others were interviewed for this film, too, men and women of varying ages and skin colors, and all were asked the same question: How would you define America? My friend, who is white, and another interviewee, a black man, gave thoughtful answers that revealed them as intellectuals. Most of the interviewees, by contrast, appeared dumbstruck by the question and sputtered what could only generously be called answers. (In fairness, these people seemed to have been stopped on the street with no warning, while the interview with my friend appeared to have taken place in her office at the university where she then taught, suggesting at least a bit of preparation.) Then there was the man whose response I recall most clearly. He was white, and in my memory he was portly with a beard and trucker's cap, though it's possible that my mind has imposed those details, which I associate with his attitude—or what I took to be his attitude, based on the little he said. "One idea: freedom," this man told the interviewers, leading me to think something along the lines of, *Ignorant motherfucker.* Without knowing this man or anything about him, I concluded that if he spoke in positive tones about the concept of freedom as it applied to America, then he was ignorant of, and no doubt indifferent to, the impediments to freedom for American citizens who don't look like him. I may have been right, and I may have been wrong; I will likely never know. But it strikes me now that, however ignorant the man may or may not have been, he touched on a very relevant matter: different people's definitions, not of America, but of freedom.

There are, it appears to me, two major disconnects regarding this. One involves the belief, on the part of much of what we'll call conservative America, a belief echoed with one or two qualifications by the people I talked to, that Americans *are* free, and thus that any measures aimed at securing rights for *certain* Americans amounts to giving such people advantages over everyone else. There is a disconnect between these attitudes and the beliefs of others, which reflect reality on the ground: continued discrimination in areas ranging from housing to employment to education to environmental safety. Bridging this disconnect might seem, then, to be a comparatively simple matter of education, of informing conservative Americans like Bob, Jack, and Fred of this reality, except for a second, and deeper, disconnect, which we might call the real one. This is the disconnect between people with the strongly held conviction that this reality must be changed at an institutional level to guarantee freedom and those with the just-as-fervent conviction that such attempts at change are antithetical to freedom itself. For freedom, in the view of this latter camp, has a flip side, which is certainly not safety and, in the end, not even fairness, but risk. To be free, say these people, is to be without a jailer but also without a caregiver. If you have a problem, *whatever that problem is*, the responsibility of dealing with it is yours. The opposite of that view, of course, is the belief that government has a basic duty to ensure, if not its citizens' well-being, then their opportunity for well-being. This real disconnect is much more difficult, and in fact may be impossible, to bridge, because what it reflects is not differences in levels of education or understanding but different concepts of morality.

Back in New York, I shared the "no jailer but no caregiver" idea via email with Jack and asked for this take on it. He wrote me: "The idea that you express…is very compelling. Sums up the way that most of us on the

Right view Freedom in America. Personal responsibility. Unfortunately, the Progressive movement has convinced about half of the population that one of the primary functions of government (make that BIG government) is to spoon feed them with benefits, programs, handouts and largesse that was originally only intended for those who, for one reason or another, could not provide for themselves. The 'Safety Net' that government must provide has been bastardized into a handout mentality that has made large numbers dependent upon big government. The Left is more than comfortable with this reality, since it buys them votes. Health Care is now to many a basic human right. That kind of muddled thinking is a result of 100 years of Progressivism. Don't get me started about Food Stamps. Anyway, your thesis on Freedom in America is thoughtful and well-stated."

A well-stated thesis, perhaps, about why the person Jack longs for — "somebody to unite us" — may be a good long time getting here.

Four

"It is what it is," people love to say these days. I used to dismiss that ubiquitous comment, probably because of its ubiquity, as being the meaningless product of lazy thought; and yet, as with many clichés, there is a kernel of wisdom in it. Acceptance of a fact — that which *is* — takes us beyond complaint and allows for action that takes that fact into account, maybe even letting us see how to use the fact to our advantage. Albert Murray might call this the blues approach. (Plus, the saying has echoes of black slang of my growing-up years: "My man, what it is.")

The idea of accepting facts applies to facts about yourself. As you get older, you come to see your own characteristics less as being virtues or faults and more as being simply part of who you are. Here is one characteristic of mine: I often don't react to things. I may hear, or overhear, a comment that would lead others in my place to fly into a rage, but I will show no sign of having heard it. This absence of response is sometimes taken for unawareness; it is not. Sometimes, things that make other people angry merely cause me to marvel, such as the day not long ago when I was walking around the campus of a southern college — where I was a visiting writer — and was stopped and questioned by an aged security guard. Other times, it takes me a while to decide that what I've heard or experienced actually is an insult.

It is what it is. I could pat myself on the back, just below my cool head, or put myself down for being slow and lacking manly anger. Or I can decide that this quality is in itself neither good nor bad and use it for what it is worth.

Take, for example, the interviews you have just read. The interviewees said a number of things that would have caused people I know to stop the question-and-answer process and start lecturing instead. My absence of a response, and my decision to ask more questions, led to more such statements. And perhaps these statements have some value — not because they are accurate, but because they provide points of inquiry. I want to look at these statements — in my unscientific way, with the feeling that they reflect what quite a few people think — and try to consider them the way that Joan Didion credited Georgia O'Keeffe with considering the world around her: "clean of received wisdom and open to what [I] see." What I see in this way leads me to three major conclusions.

It is not news that Trump's presidential campaign and election clearly emboldened many who hate or resent people of color. I am not particularly concerned with the reasons they feel that way. A white man who hates me because I am black is beyond my reach, and my life is too short for me to worry about what he thinks. But my conversations with other kinds of white people, and my readings of books such as *Strangers in Their Own Land*, by Arlie Russell Hochschild, who interviewed scads of conservative whites in the Louisiana bayou area — people reluctant to express racist views, whether or not they hold them — point to a different sort of attitude toward blacks and other minorities that may be as common as, if not more common than, hatred or contempt or resentment; it is an attitude that transcends concerns of race, that may be said to be any person's attitude toward those to whom she is not close:

Indifference.

For example: black people get a bad rap for being antigay. I have seen no evidence that blacks are any more antigay than any other group, but try going up to a random black heterosexual and saying, "Hey, you coming to the gay pride rally?" The answer, likely as not, would be, "Why?" Not hatred, not necessarily prejudice. Indifference.

I am not a pet owner. I am mortally allergic to cats, and for a number of reasons I have never owned a dog. Over the years I have been fond of a few pets belonging to friends, but those attachments have been few and far between. I certainly bear animals no ill will, and if I ever saw an animal being needlessly tortured, I like to think I would put a stop to it, or try to. Still, I eat meat. Happily, eagerly. I have given up trying to justify this, even to myself—not that I ever tried very hard—because the arguments make no sense. The simple, not very pretty truth is that while I have nothing against animals, I do not care enough about them to join PETA or stop eating meat or buying leather. The best word for my attitude is indifference. When I have tried to justify eating meat, though, my arguments produce the same aroma of fresh, hot bullshit that drifts up from Bob's words as he tries to defend Trump for not distancing himself from the Ku Klux Klan. *You have to deal with the circumstances. The Ku Klux Klan or any other organization out there is what it is. And every president, whether you're a woman, a man, black or white or brown or whatever, they're confronted with the same ideologies... Why would he distance himself from the Ku Klux Klan and not from another group?* (And, actually, Bob's question is a good one, though not for the reason he thinks. Why, indeed, would Trump distance himself from the KKK's endorsement, having called it forth with his dog whistles?)

Jack allowed as how Trump ought to have taken "two giant steps, maybe three" from the Klan endorsement—but the fact that he didn't was no barrier to Jack's voting for Trump. Jack is mostly indifferent to the issue, as he frankly admits to having been indifferent to the civil rights movement (*the civil rights movement wasn't really big on my radar because it didn't really involve me*) and the women's movement: *Let's take your point that men have an unfair advantage over women in the workplace and let's agree to that. Now why would I, as a man, want to change that?* Similarly, Fred, from Missouri, is indifferent to Trump's crotch-grabbing boast.

There is indifference, and, secondly, there is ignorance. This extends to ignorance of one's own negative attitudes (see Bob's "jibber-jabber-jive"), a problem that is not limited to conservatives. And while it has become conventional wisdom that Americans in different geographical regions and of different political persuasions get radically different spins on news stories — or even different news altogether — some of the views of the people I spoke with not only confirm that theory but hint at the dangers of this ever-increasing trend. "I don't think he's uncivil," Bob told me about Trump, a comment to which I don't know where to begin responding — and to which, fortunately, a response would be superfluous.

An unsettling effect of all this is that people like Bob, Jack, and Fred appear to view the troubles facing poor communities of color as being legacies of slavery and its attendant racism — which, of course, in numerous ways, they are — but also to view those legacies as being perpetuated *mainly by the communities themselves*, not by the same racism that allowed slavery to flourish and made the century following Emancipation nearly as difficult for many black people as had the "peculiar institution" itself. To be ignorant of the effects of such racism is to view people of color as victims of their own backwardness. Together, indifference and ignorance erect a virtual wall between the concerns of white Americans and those of their black and brown counterparts.

Let's take a look at a few of those concerns. Before I conducted the interviews, I, like the next (liberal) guy, had heard about educational inequity, but I had not read, for example, Gillian B. White's September 30, 2015, *Atlantic* article on findings by the data scientist David Mosenkis: that in Pennsylvania, while more state funding goes to poor school districts than to rich ones—as it is supposed to—a breakdown of school districts revealed that the whiter the school district, the more money it received, regardless of poverty level, making for a racial imbalance mirrored in various ways all around the country. Like the next guy, I had heard about continued employment discrimination, but I had not seen the 2013 study showing that when 9,400 fake resumes were submitted online for job openings, the resumes with black-sounding names were 16 percent less likely than others to generate calls for interviews. (A 2016 study showed an absence of bias, but that was after first names like Kamau and Taniqua were taken out and last names like Washington and Jefferson—which many do not know belong overwhelmingly to black people—were put in.) Like the next guy, I had seen coverage of shootings of blacks by police officers, but I had not read the *Washington Post* data revealing that while police fatally shoot more whites than blacks, when the percentage of blacks in the general population (13 percent) is taken into account, blacks are 2.5 times as likely as whites to be shot to death by police, and an unarmed black person is five times as likely as his white counterpart to suffer that fate. (Perhaps it is true — as asserted by the men who would not be interviewed by me — that there has not been an increase in police shootings of blacks. Perhaps things were *always* this bad. Is that better, guys?) Like the next guy, I strongly suspected that police mistreatment of blacks was a bigger problem than could be posed by "a few bad apples," but I had not opened the 2017 book *Chokehold*, by Paul Butler, a former federal prosecutor, who writes, "Virtually every objective investigation of a U.S. law enforcement agency finds that the police, *as policy*, treat African Americans with contempt." Like the next guy, I knew that Donald Trump, to put it kindly, had a tendency to bend the truth, but I had not heard his outrageous claim that blacks are responsible for 81 percent of killings of white Americans. (The truth is that whites are killed mostly by other whites, blacks by other blacks.)

Just as harmful as indifference to and/or lack of access to such information is active resistance to its implications, and seen in that light, the interviews I did not conduct are as revealing as those I did. Peter — who, based on the wording of my email message, refused to be interviewed — illustrates such resistance perfectly. His response demonstrates what appears to me to be a strong need *not* to believe in the truth of the adversity people of color encounter, the question then becoming what accounts for that need. A reasonable guess — and the third factor I would identify — would be denial, arising from the desire to avoid feelings of guilt, feelings that would be present in this instance if one is rooted in the idea of one's own whiteness.

And yet the power of pure ignorance should not be underestimated. To be ignorant of the continued force of racism in American life is to have tunnel vision, seeing a thing but missing what is going on around it. Barack Obama, Jack said to me, was "a little bit" responsible for racism's having gotten worse, and the example he gave was Obama's initial response to the arrest of Henry Louis Gates, which was: "I don't know, not having been there and not seeing all the facts, what role race played in that. But I think it's fair to say, number 1, any of us would be pretty angry; number 2, that the Cambridge police acted stupidly in arresting somebody when there was already proof that they were in their own home; and number 3, what I think we know separate and apart from this incident is there is a long history in this country of African Americans and Latinos being stopped by police disproportionately. That's just a fact." Obama later said that he "could've calibrated those words differently," but take "stupidly" out of his remarks, and what is left is fact. But

Jack's view—based in ignorance—is that "we've moved out of the arena where segregation and racism have that much of an impact," so much so that, as Jack sees it, the greatest disservice a president can do with regard to racism is to remind us of its existence, to reopen supposedly old wounds. This is like condemning the use of the flu vaccine—condemning the very use of the word "flu"—when a third of the country has called in sick.

A former MFA student of mine, Angelique Stevens, herself a professor of literature and philosophy, put me onto the Holocaust scholar Lawrence Langer's concept of the "disappeared criminal" in Holocaust literature—that is, the tendency to focus on what victims of the Holocaust did, sometimes to one another, in order to survive, while those who had put them in that position remain hidden. The same concept can be applied to impoverished black and brown neighborhoods. Based on the answers to my questions about who is to blame for conditions in these areas, Bob and Jack, in particular, seem to me to think that poor blacks perpetuate patterns of bad behavior that may initially have been set in motion by outside forces but that continue today because people in those communities simply don't know any better. So to vote for Trump, in their view, would not be to vote for the disappeared criminal, since, as far as Jack and Bob know, there is no such figure.

But let us poke around for some other places where that criminal may have disappeared to.

Mishi Faruqee, my fellow Brooklynite, is the wife of my cousin Amadou Diallo (who shares a name with the unarmed African immigrant gunned down by police in 1999). Mishi, well-known in her field as an advocate for juveniles in the criminal justice system, put me in touch with a woman named Jeannette Bocanegra. Jeannette works as the director of family engagement at Community Connections for Youth, a nonprofit organization in the South Bronx whose mission, as stated on its Web site, is "to empower grassroots faith and neighborhood organizations to develop effective community driven alternatives to incarceration for youth." I contacted Jeannette about visiting her at the Community Connections offices.

East 149th Street in the South Bronx, near where it intersects with the Grand Concourse, has the feel at once of a poor neighborhood and one that is on the move (though when I tried to put my finger on what, besides the total absence of white people, made it seem poor, I came up with very little). The buildings of Eugenio María De Hostos Community College of the City University of New York dominate the intersection where you come up out of the subway from the number 5 train—that, and an enormous post office; heading east on 149th, you cross an overpass above Metro-North train tracks and pass banks, various stores, and no shortage of fast-food restaurants. On the seventh floor of a relatively tall building that shoots up between an office supply store on the left and a bank on the right, I found

Jeannette Bocanegra. She is pleasant-faced, with graying hair — what looked to be a great deal of it — peeking out from under a head wrap; she wore a white top, black slacks, gray slippers, and a necklace and earrings made of the same black, not-expensive-looking material. After checking with the receptionist, she took me into a small room.

Jeannette — who said I should use her real name — has a down-to-earth air that made me like her immediately. She was born to Puerto Rican parents in the South Bronx, where she was raised; as a child she went back and forth to Puerto Rico. Her mother married a man with four children, after which the couple had Jeannette and her three younger siblings. Jeannette herself is a mother of six. Her oldest child is thirty. Because she faced what she called "challenges in the schools" she attended in her youth, she has spent the last twenty-plus years working with families in schools, who experience the same "lack of resources and support in the community" that she encountered. She described her work as "my life, my passion." She began organizing in the community, "reaching out to families so they can get involved in their children's education." While Jeannette does not herself have a lot of formal education — she spent a year and a half in college — she completed certificate programs in youth training, youth development, and cultural sensitivity; she has trained as a facilitator of interactions between families and various bureaucracies.

"Take me through a typical day or a typical week in your work," I said to Jeannette.

"A typical day? It varies. This is not a nine-to-five, Monday-through-Friday type of work. A typical morning as I'm getting ready may be getting a text or a phone call from a parent. 'My child does not want to wake up to go to school.'" The problem at that point, she said—beyond the child's not wanting to go to school—is that the child's absence will "involve various systems" in the family's home. "We know that 99.9 percent of the time, when a young person is being truant, they threaten the families with the child welfare system."

"Who does? Who threatens?"

"Personnel at the school. This kid is not coming to school for a certain amount of days. We're not asking why. We don't know why. There has to be a why! It's not just that this kid just woke up and overnight decided that 'I don't want to go to that school anymore.' *Something happened*. So families, because they have other children at home, they say, 'We're not going to allow one kid to jeopardize the rest.'" That is, one child skipping school can bring the Administration for Children's Services (ACS) down on the whole family, which is how families get broken up. Sometimes, Jeannette says, rather than allowing that to happen, a parent will say to a child who has missed school, "If you don't want to go to school I'm going to put a PINS." PINS stands for Persons in Need of Supervision; a parent can write a PINS request to have family court involved in controlling a child when nothing else has worked. And, Jeannette said, the family is "not looking to kind of penalize or punish the kid; they're just looking for help.

"So just because of fear of having all those systems involved, those are the calls that I get. 'My kid don't want to go to school and I don't want to get penalized. I don't want to go back to court. I don't want to go deal with the child welfare system. The school keeps threatening me with ACS.' It's just so much that families are dealing with, and that can be a typical morning for me. And I'm knocking on the family's door at 6:30 in the morning, saying, 'Where is the child at? Is he in the room? Can I speak to him?'"

"So in your experience," I said, "when a child doesn't want to go to school, what are the reasons?"

"It might be a safety issue and they don't want to talk about it."

"So the kid could just get beat up at school, that kind of thing?"

"Yes. And there's no one they can trust in the school. Maybe they're not doing that well academically and don't want to feel ashamed because they can't compete with the work. So there are various reasons why."

"When you think about the community as a whole," I said, "what do you see as the biggest challenges facing the families in the community?"

"The lack of investment."

"On the part of…?"

"Of city/state government."

"Investment in what?"

"In education. In social programs. And even private funders that have a heart and say, you know, these young people are smart. They're talented, they're gifted, but we're not investing in them."

"Do you feel like there are things that the community itself could do that are not being done? Or do you feel like the main problem is the lack of investment in programs?"

"You know, I look at what's being invested in incarcerating and housing young people in detention centers versus what's being invested in schools and after-school programs and even jobs during the summer for young people. It's not even the amount of money; it's more on the punishment and penalizing and not strengthening the skills that young people have. Because we have a *smart* generation. I think we have the smartest generation, but we're not tapping into their strength and into those skills that they have." She referred to watching young people texting: "I mean, who can move their fingers so fast? And they multitask! I can't—I tell people I can't even sometimes walk and chew gum at that same time." She laughed, heartily. "But these young people, they can multitask. You see that lady that fell in Jersey? She was texting and walking and kind of tripped and she hurt herself. A young person wouldn't be like that."

I laughed. Then I asked, "What are some surprising things that your work has taught you?"

"That racism really exists." Though, she added, "I knew it did."

"What are some examples?"

"The schools. I'm going to say when something horrible happens in a school. In one of our schools it would be, 'Let's put more police in the schools. They need more metal detectors.'"

"So by 'something horrible'," I said, "you mean somebody gets..."

"Somebody is shot or something happens that's maybe a little horrible. But then when it happens in a more white, affluent school, it's like, 'Let's put more counselors, let's put in more of the social and emotional components to support the kids.' And with our kids it's like more policing. 'Let's impose these new laws.' Those are some of the things that are not fair, and we always say there's more young people of color incarcerated versus white kids. I'm not saying, okay, arrest more white kids and make it even, but just be fair. Treat our kids the same way. Be fair."

"I don't know the statistics, but if somebody says to you, look, people in communities of color commit a disproportionate number of crimes, therefore there need to be more police, what would you say to that?"

"*No*. It's the same way that I shared with you about the schools. If you put in more of the social and emotional components of what young people in communities need, then you will see less of [the crime] you normally see on TV. You know they're always promoting or showing what kids are doing that's not right. But there's more that are doing great things and we're not showcasing the great things that young people are doing.

"I was watching the [Puerto Rican Day] Parade yesterday, and you know a lot of young people were marching and a lot of young activists and young people are doing *great* things. So let's kind of invest in the ones that are giving us a run for our money. And we're all different and we all need a different level of support. Some might need more care than others, and it's the same way with our kids. One might need more than the next one."

"When I was in California," I told Jeannette, "I was talking to this guy who voted for Trump and we were talking about communities of color out there, and he was talking about black communities and Latino communities, and he said that to him the difference seemed to be that the black communities did not want to succeed. How would you respond to that?"

Jeannette looked mildly offended. "It's the same way when someone tells me parents don't care. I'm like, *no*. Every parent cares. Every parent wants their child to succeed, but sometimes we don't know how and what to do. I mean, if we're not given certain skills towards certain things, we don't know how. You know, I have parents who never received a hug growing up. So how can I want to give you a hug if I don't know what it is to give a hug?

How can I want to do certain things if I wasn't taught those things? So everyone wants to succeed but we just need those skills and those tools and that motivation. But no one wants to fail."

I said, "Are there times when you think, 'I wish people in my community would do this, or work harder on this, or…'"

"I sometimes see myself saying things like: I wish that line that's there in front of Foot Locker for these sneakers that are just coming out—why don't we have a line like this when we have a school meeting or a community meeting or a listening session?"

(I think here of a passage from George Orwell's book *The Road to Wigan Pier*, about poor industrial workers in the north of England in the 1930s: "[T]hey don't necessarily lower their standards by cutting out luxuries and concentrating on necessities; more often it is the other way around—the more natural way, if you come to think of it…You may have three halfpence in your pocket and not a prospect in the world, and only the corner of a leaky bedroom to go home to; but in your new clothes you can stand on the street corner indulging in a private daydream of yourself as Clark Gable or Greta Garbo, which compensates you for a great deal.")

"But I think," Jeannette was saying, "it's how society has kind of shaped the thinking of a lot of our young people that looking good on the outside is more important than what's inside. I say to my young people, it's better to have a dressed mind than a dressed body. Sometimes I catch myself saying things like that when I see these long lines. And then I also see lines with" — she sighed heavily — "families and shopping carts to get food [donations]. And I'm like, how is that happening in such a rich country?"

"Do you feel like the situations within families cause a lot of problems that you see?"

"The lack of *support* for families. I always say this is modern day slavery."

"How so?"

"How so? By separating families" — the way that slavery separated members of black families. "Systems that are separating families."

"What's an example?"

"Incarceration is a great example. Removing kids from home. I've always said the child welfare system has always been removing and separating families because of bad parents. 'Let's save the kids. Let's move them to a better place.' And a large percentage of those decisions... Young people say that when they were removed, 'The places they sent me to were way worse than the one they took me from.' Incarceration, removing individuals and young kids because they are horrible and they don't belong in the community. And the further they are, the likelihood of family visits kind of fades away."

At this point I thought of what Bob said to me: *Those kids, probably the best thing that ever happened to them is getting away from their mom and dad and the inner city and going someplace else, and live with even black people outside of the inner city. Put them with white people outside the inner city and they will become a better person for themselves and for our country.*

"So," I said to Jeannette, "crimes in the community—why do they get committed?"

"Maybe a need. To take care of a need that you may have. It might be an addiction. It might be to take care of your family. But there is a need. I cannot pinpoint what their personal need is, but there's a need."

"Okay. If you could make everybody in the country understand one or two things, or several things, what would you make everybody in the country understand?"

"That we might dress different."

"'We' meaning…?"

"Different folks from different socioeconomic status. We might look different, we might speak a different language but we're all human. We all want the best for our children. We all want to live comfortably. We want to be able to contribute to society. I'm not saying give me a handout"—I thought of Jack here: *a handout mentality that has made large numbers dependent upon big government*—"but just treat me fair. And provide us with the necessary tools. Not everything is dealt with a hammer. So just provide us with the necessary tools and then we can sustain and take care of ourselves. I mean the systems are doing what they were meant to do, so I would say demolish the system. And if you're going to create it, create it where it's more supportive to the community and it's uplifting the community, not — not a punitive and paternalistic way of dealing with the community. It's more of a partnership. Families care. But we're not investing in families.

"I'm not sure if I answered the question about, you know, the young person who does not want to wake up to go to school and sometimes we don't ask why. We don't visit the school to find out why." Jeannette said she has had luck "negotiating" with young people. "Like, 'Okay, try and go to school three days.' I'm going to go to the kid's school. I'm going to find out why he doesn't want to go. 'Let's see if you can connect at least with one person that whenever you're feeling a little down then that person can kind of give you that one-to-one attention.'"

"And when you've done that, has it worked?"

"Yeah. Because I don't give up. I know that doing it one time…You've got to continue. It's like teaching your children how to walk. The first try, you're not going to give up. Then once they start walking you applaud them and you start making phone calls. 'Guess what! My baby's walking!'"

* * *

As one who had begun to reexamine his feelings about being black and identifying with America, that land that has so mistreated people who look like me, who had begun to feel, if not wrong, then very alone in my determination to judge everyone individually, I was intrigued when I learned of the existence of the National African American Gun Association. The term "African American" — with or without a hyphen — has been in common use now for a generation or more, and yet seeing it in this context led me to consider it anew. Saying the term with awareness, expressing an identification in times like these with Africa *and* with America, seems to me almost a radical act, one that dares others to call it a contradiction; calling oneself a citizen of that land — America — that is currently showing its worst face to its citizens and the world, and at the same time evoking the spirit of Africa, so hated and mocked by those who consider themselves the "real" Americans: Is it an act of confusion, of self-hatred? Or is it an act of defiance, a way of saying, "This is my country, too, whatever I may have suffered here"? Why "African" rather than "black"? Does that choice speak to an affiliation beyond what we have known on these shores, this land that is nonetheless so much a part of us? Throw into the mix the word "gun," with its suggestion of unapologetic self-defense, and things get interesting indeed.

And so I felt compelled to speak with the founder and president of this organization, whose name is Philip Smith. I contacted Smith and arranged to see him in Atlanta, where he lives, on a Friday in late July 2017. My flight got in at 10:25 a.m.; hurrying through the airport with my briefcase and overnight bag in search of the taxi stand, I skidded on some spilled coffee and nearly took a spill myself, coming down so hard on my left foot that I aggravated my already iffy knee. In the taxi I texted Smith to say that I might be a few minutes late for our 11:15 meeting but was en route. He texted back to say that he had been unavoidably detained but would be at the agreed-upon meeting place — Stoddard's Range and Guns — in about an hour. I arrived, as it happened, on the dot, but now I had quite a bit of time to kill.

Stoddard's Range and Guns is housed in a low brick building, its name in big blue letters on an enormous white background, with images of two bullets to the left of the letters — one bullet pointing this way, one that way. The inside resembled your neighborhood discount store, with this difference: the aisles contained not coloring books and nail polish remover but pistols and ammunition, and under a long glass case at the back were enough rifles to launch the D-Day invasion. Beyond the rifles, behind closed doors, was the firing range, from which came the muffled sound of gunshots.

I saw four people working there, all men, three white, one black. The youthful-looking Patrick, one of the white guys, was the manager. When I explained that I was there to meet Philip Smith, who would be late, Patrick let me put my things in the Titanium Lounge, a long, comfortable room for guests, with chairs and sofas. With nearly an hour to amuse myself, I set out in search of lunch.

Stray beyond New York City, and America is just not made for pedestrians. I was told by two people on the street that I would find "a ton of restaurants" at nearby Atlantic Station shopping center, but no amount of walking seemed to bring this fabled shopping center any closer. The heat and humidity, meanwhile, made me feel as if someone had submerged a sheet in warm water and then wrapped me in it, and my left knee was issuing complaints about the near-spill in the airport and the fifty-odd years of being abused in various ways and generally taken for granted before that. Finally, I found a Starbucks, nearly hurt myself wolfing down a sausage, egg, and cheese sandwich the temperature of fresh lava, then headed back out into the heat. By the time I made it back to the Titanium Lounge, I looked as if I had been hosed, and I felt unpresentable, and old.

My spirits lifted when Philip Smith walked in. He was accompanied by his brother, Vincent—who, like Philip, as I was to learn, is a transplant from the West Coast and works in human resources. Their friendliness put me at ease. Philip, a strong-looking fifty-eight-year-old with a shaved head and carefully trimmed mustache, wore jeans, sandals, and a short-sleeved blue polo shirt with white stripes. While Vincent sat quietly on one sofa, I took another, and Philip sat near me in a chair.

He comes from a blue-collar family and was born and raised, he told me, in Vallejo, in Northern California, about thirty miles up from San Francisco and Oakland.

He describes the neighborhood where he grew up as being very diverse: "Primarily African American, but we had Latinos, we had an Asian mix. A lot of Filipinos in Vallejo...We used to go play with black kids. We played with Asian kids. We played with white kids." After graduating from high school in 1977 — the era of "bell bottoms, big 'fros, jheri curls, all that good stuff" — he attended UC Davis, getting his degree in 1984. He enrolled in the Bank of America training program ("which I loved until I found out I hated banking") and then tried real estate for a time before finding his way to HR and recruiting. "That's where I made a lot of my money, working Silicon Valley, doing contracts. I'm a headhunter and that's what I do." He started his own company in 2007.

Meanwhile, five years earlier, he had moved to Atlanta. "Moved my whole family, wife, kids, and everything," he told me. "And I came here because I wanted a different kind of experience. I wanted my kids to see blacks in a very positive role. I came here and it's been everything that I imagined.

"One day after work — at that time I was working for somebody else — two guys said, 'Hey, do you want to go shoot at the range?' I said, 'I don't think I want to do that kind of crap.' And he goes, 'Man, I want you to come.' I said no. They said, 'Come on, man.' They literally pulled me to go. So I went to another range — not this one — and had a good time, man. Loved it. In fact, I liked it so much that I said, 'You guys coming here next week?'

They said yeah, so I met them again, and had a really good time.

"But the one thing I noticed, when I went there, is that there were no African Americans there, nobody who looked like me. And I said to myself: if I could be having such a good time, I know other African Americans could be having a great time, too. So that kind of got the light-bulb almost on.

"But even though I was having a very good time, I noticed that I got some looks in there. They didn't say anything, but they gave me that 'Boy, what are you doing here?' type of look, and I didn't like that. And I said, you know what? I'm going to start an organization where we can come collectively together and have a good time and feel comfortable. That's when I went home, started to do the research."

Philip launched the NAAGA in February 2015. Today the association, which is open to all but is "unapologetically African American," has thirty-seven chapters and twenty thousand members. Asked to define the primary aim of the organization, Philip said, "Safety is the main thing," and added, "a lot of the folks that come through the door might have a gun sitting in their attic for the last ten years. Their daddy gave it to them. Their mother, great grandfather. It just sits there. So they think they have a gun to protect themselves but they actually don't. Because under pressure, under duress more importantly, how are you going to act when somebody's busting through your door, coming at you and your wife? You're going to be fumbling with the gun because you don't remember. They don't have what we call muscle memory. Our job is to make sure that you have a high level of competence with that firearm under pressure." Philip said — to my enormous relief — that he favors background checks for gun purchases, but he added, "You can't legislate morality." ("I'm carrying now," he told me — that is, he had a weapon on him as we spoke.) He told me that on founding the NAAGA, he received hate mail from blacks and whites, though mostly from whites, much of it including racial slurs.

What separates his organization from others of its kind, Philip said, is that the NAAGA fosters discussions on issues such as "driving while black" and the killings of Trayvon Martin and Philando Castile. "So we talked about" Castile's being fatally shot by a police officer, Philip said, "and the thing that really helped folks in our community is that they were able to vent. Some people just wanted to curse. Some people wanted to talk intelligently. Some people had an emotional catharsis. Whatever that case is, you're allowed to do that."

Philip told me that he is "conservative by nature," that he is a registered Republican who is "just very pro-family" and "a very pro-life person." He also told me that he voted for Hillary Clinton.

That brought me to what I had really flown to Atlanta to ask this man.

"How would you describe the relationship of blacks to America?"

"I think, overall, blacks, in terms of relating to America—it's kind of twisted," Philip said. Intentionally or not, he echoed Chris Rock here: "It's like being raised by your uncle who is a pedophile who has molested you. But he still loves you. You know? He's gotten you to that point where you're eighteen but he's molested you for years and years and now you're supposed to walk out there and not have any handicap or any issues. So it can be twisted for some. For some it's a very positive, very good experience, and for a lot it's been tough. It's been very tough economically, being in rough areas, not having a good education. I was lucky. We had great education coming up, so we were among the kids who can walk in any room and hold our own with anyone. But a lot of folks didn't have that experience."

"Do you consider yourself an American?"

"Yeah. Every day. Every day."

"Has anything ever happened to threaten your commitment to being an American or your identification with America?"

"No. No. But also I will say this. There are certain people out there that want to degrade your Americanness. That can be somebody at a job or somebody walking down the street. Interaction with some law enforcement—not all, but some, because most law enforcement people that I talk to are doing a great job. Ninety percent of those guys are doing a great job, guys and gals. But there are some people out there who want to put you down to pull themselves up."

I asked if Trump's election had led him to reconsider any of his notions about being an American as a black person.

"No it doesn't. I think the larger question is why did these people who have questionable views collectively vote for Trump?"

"So," I said, "Trump's election makes you question what they're doing, not what you're doing." He agreed.

"You are an American," I said. "Why do you consider yourself an American versus considering yourself an African on US soil?"

"Culturally, I was born and raised here, and there is a distinct African American experience that is very, very different. If I go into Ethiopia or Ghana, do I love those brothers there? Absolutely. But we've had different experiences and different languages. We have different beliefs. Not that it's bad or good on either side, but it's different. All of us are a product of our life experiences culturally, economically, and it comes fused in this person called a human being here in America. So yes, I feel very, very American! If that's the question."

"This might be a trick question," I said. "Do you feel culturally you have more in common with a white American or with an African, for example?"

"Culturally, I — it depends on the African, but generally speaking most white folks who have been raised here with me? Probably, culturally, I would say yeah, we have a lot in common. But let me be distinct on this. I have a kinship, beyond your normal interaction, with anybody from the African continent. I say this and it kind of gives you an indication of the kind of person I am: there are two kinds of black men in America—to me. There are those who have made it in spite of being black, and there are those who have made it because they are black. I have made it because I am black. The intelligence that I have, the strength that I have in my body, the background from which I come is from Africa and that has been given to me from my forefathers. You've probably heard the term 'I stand on my forefathers' shoulders.' That's what I am about." (Those who succeed in spite of being black, he said, are those "who don't have a connection to their heritage or their people" and are in a position to help others but don't.)

"In the essence of who I am every day," Philip said, "I'm just very pro-black, very unapologetically. Do I talk about it a lot? No. But if you ask me sitting down and having a conversation, I believe that that's the reason why I'm here and the reason why I'm able to think the way I'm able to think at the high level that I'm able to do it. It's because of my forefathers."

"From Africa," I said.

"Absolutely."

"And traditions passed down?"

"I'm not going to say traditions because a lot of our traditions have been cut. I mean, obviously, if you ask me do I speak any of the African languages? I would say no. Do I speak Swahili? No. But for me there is a spiritual connection that I have when I talk to them and that was given to me as a child. My parents would say be proud of who you are. Be proud of your forefathers who fought for you in America and those who are in Africa, and that really stuck with me as a child. I'm very, very proud of that fact."

"Can you define that spirituality?"

"It's a feeling. When I sit there and talk to someone from a different country in Africa, if I'm talking to a brother from Ghana, to me it's an enjoyable conversation because I have that feeling, that spiritual connection that we have with one another."

"That sort of indefinable kind of connection?"

"I'll give you an example. It is like a Jewish person going back to Israel. They don't speak Hebrew. They've been raised here in America, but when they go there, they have this sense of connection. That's the same connection I have when I talk to somebody who is from Africa, or hopefully when I go to Africa I'll have that connection."

At this point I recalled having been asked by more than one white person why American blacks so insist on an identification with Africa — why, even, we use the term "African American." Is it, these whites wanted to know, because we thought we were better than others? The

138

answer, of course, is no. It is the result of having been told, in countless ways, that we're not *as good* as others, that we and our culture are not valued here in the land of our birth. And so the response is to seek another land, one that is, if only in our minds, more welcoming, and to say *not* "I am better than you" but "I have a culture as good, a history as rich, as yours."

"Do you feel," I said, "like there are things that the African American community can do that it is not doing to alleviate the problems we face? Or is the vast, vast majority of what we face just situational and institutional?"

"That's a multilayered question—multilayered answer. There are so many things that we are facing right now. Lack of fathers in the home. Over-incarceration. Lack of job opportunities. It is many things. This is my take. If you take any group of people—let's look at Chicago, 'cause Chicago is the Baby of the Year. Those brothers have inferior education. Schools are horrible. They are not really schools, they're training grounds for correctional officers. Two, you put them in an environment where they have no economic opportunity. They come out of high school with no skills. Three, on top of all that you put them in a very confrontational relationship with the law enforcement officers. You over-incarcerate them so by the time they are twenty-two or twenty-three they have two or three felonies on them. They can't get a job. They have families to take care of because they have babies. They have women that they have relationships with. What would you do in that situation if you could not get a job, you're stigmatized already with the felony? What are you going to do to take care of your family?"

"Sell drugs."

"You're gonna sell drugs or you're gonna rob people, or do both. But the one thing I think we need to start doing is realizing that we have to collectively start working together. Because every other community, every other ethnic group is working aggressively together."

"You mean within their own communities."

"Within their own communities, to survive. There's an economic component to that. If I'm of an Asian or Latino hue, I know that I have a responsibility to go to an Asian cleaners or go to an Asian attorney — and we don't do that. Our money is gone within, like, six hours of when we cash our checks, and that's something that has to stop. If we support each other, that will be a much better scenario for us as a people."

I said, "If you could convey — if there were one or two messages that you could convey to all African Americans, what do you think they would be?"

"Be confident," Philip said. "Believe that you have the right. You are not a discounted citizen. You have the right to purchase arms to protect your family. It is not a social stigma. You would not believe the amount of men that I talk to on a daily basis — and we're talking doctors, lawyers, black professionals who have PhDs who call me directly and say, 'Hey Phil. I want to get a gun but I just don't know how I'm going to be perceived as a black person who is a doctor if I get a gun.' I always tell them, 'You're an American citizen, right? What's the problem?' You've earned that right. Your forefathers have died many times over for you to get to this point, for me to get to this point. So what's the problem? And it comes down to confidence also. You have to believe that it's okay. And stop worrying about — and this is something I always tell my kids — 'Don't worry about what people think of you. You worry about what you think of yourself and that will take care of everything else.'"

* * *

As it turned out, and as I should have known, I could not simply walk into the range at Stoddard's and start shooting at targets; I would have to have instruction first. I was debating with myself about that when the matter was decided for me. I asked one of the workers if he knew the number of a car service I could call when I was ready to leave, but he didn't; that raised the question of how I — apparently the last US citizen without an Uber or Lyft app on his phone — would get to my hotel. But Philip, who was leaving at that moment, kindly offered to give me a ride. Walking out with him and Vincent, I took a last look back at Stoddard's, where an idea had taken hold, one I would pursue.

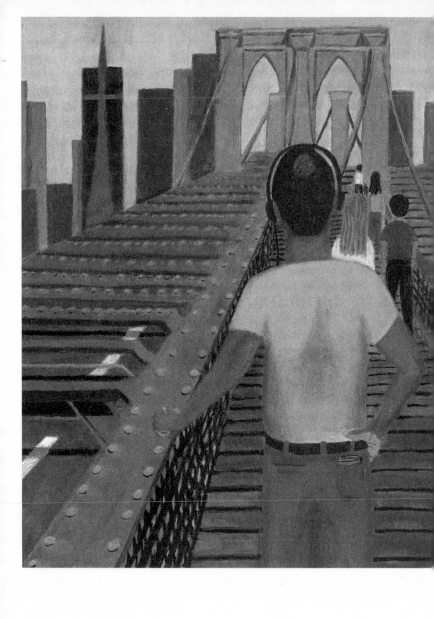

Five

Where does all of this leave me?

Since Trump's election, I have been in somewhat the same position as the priest who has lost his faith. I don't know if I feel bereft of that faith — my belief in my Americanness, in judging others individually — because I have walked away from it, or because it has betrayed me, or if either of those things has actually happened; I don't know if we've undergone something like a trial separation. Maybe, come to think of it, marriage is a better metaphor: I feel something akin to what longtime spouses feel after they fight — anger but also a sense of aloneness, of things being wrong, regardless of who is right.

Like most couples after a fight, I long to reconnect, but also to keep sight of what has caused the break.

Look at them out there, all those expressions, physical and verbal, of antiblack feeling, filling the air like those hordes of flying monkeys in *The Wizard of Oz* that so terrified me when I was a child, only in this case I can't tell myself that they're not real. Some white people care and want to help, and some are helping; many white people resent us or out-and-out hate us; and many others, maybe most, are indifferent, not actively wishing us ill but in the end not giving a damn — an uninformed or misinformed lot led by criminally slanted news coverage and cynical politicians to vote against my interests and, in many cases, their own. This does not seem a good basis for a positive attitude toward those who make up the majority in the country with which I have chosen to identify. Reason continues to dictate that I should not make up my mind about a person, any person, based on what he looks like. But at what point is reason unreasonable?

Look at it, the government of the country with which I have chosen to identify: doing its best, beginning under then–Attorney General Jefferson Beauregard Sessions III, to knock down what remains of protections against police brutality, voter discrimination, and prison sentences ridiculously and tragically out of proportion to drug offenses (to say nothing of what has happened to families at the border). Look at the police force that is charged with enforcing the country's laws, that sometimes seems to have openly declared war on black people. *The systems are doing what they were meant to do*, as Jeannette Bocanegra put it.

But then look at it, the number of blacks who are killed each year, and at who kills them. Sources differ — why? — about the number of black people killed by police; to pick one recent year, 2015, an average figure from those sources is around three hundred. For some reason (and the reason would make for an interesting line of inquiry all by itself), there is more agreement over the number of times blacks killed each other that same year: 2,380. Let us choose for now to accept that figure, and let us agree that it is horrifying. Much of that can be attributed to crime stemming from lack of opportunity. Frankly, I do not believe all of it can be. Some of it has to be skewed values, reflecting to a great extent — *concentrating* — the values of the larger society of which black people are a part. I do not know the answer to repairing or instilling values, but I can say, with a great deal of confidence, what the answer is not: separating families through Child Services, as Jeannette Bocanegra mentioned, or through racially biased incarceration, as Michelle Alexander has detailed so thoroughly.

As I sit writing this, nothing seems more clear, more urgent, than the need to sort all of this out, to find a way to protect people of color from both our enemies and ourselves.

Of course, I have felt similar urgency before.

In the early 2000s, when The Pie was in elementary school and Louie in day care, I began thinking about how I might help kids of color who did not have all the advantages my kids had. We were not rich by any means, but we were doing okay, living in a rent-stabilized building in our upscale, mostly white neighborhood where, by pure luck, my kids were zoned for possibly the best public elementary school in Brooklyn. It occurred to me that I might not have to look far for what I sought. Most kids in the school lived close by, but a few were from poorer areas a neighborhood or two away. Those kids already had access to a quality formal education, of course, but so much of what makes for success in the classroom is found at home: two parents with time to read with their children instead of a single parent who has to work two jobs to hold her family together; books and ideas in the very air you breathe. So I approached the administrators at my daughters' school and told them, simply, that I wanted to help.

That was how I was put in touch with a black third-grader I will call Jamal. He lived in an apartment with his mother, whom I'll call Darlene, about a fifteen- or twenty-minute walk from where I lived. On weekends I went to their place to help Jamal with reading. I soon discovered that the job I had taken on was smaller than I had thought and also much, much bigger. My fantasy, I think now, was to work with a kid who was hungry to learn but who struggled; I would sit patiently with him, helping as he developed the skills he would need to read for pleasure and to learn about things he was interested in, and we would both feel great about his progress. Jamal, as it turned out, was not a bad reader at all, and he wondered aloud — and understandably — why he had to devote a chunk of his weekend to these lessons when he would rather be doing things that did not involve me. I began to wonder that myself. Darlene supplied the answer. We were talking in her kitchen one afternoon when she told me, "Someone needs to teach him to be a man. I can't teach him that."

Jamal was smart, and not just when it came to reading. He seemed to sense things, even when he didn't put them into words — though he often did put them into words, to devastating effect — and one of the things he seemed to sense was that he had gotten a raw deal in life. I didn't ask, and was never told, what the situation with Jamal's father was, but I imagine that fatherlessness was a major entry in his mental ledger of ways the world had wronged him, and my name appeared in one or two places in that scrupulously kept book, too. One Sunday shortly before Christmas of 2001, at Jamal's apartment, Darlene gave me a thirty dollar American Express gift card. The following week I gave Jamal a present: a fifteen dollar gift card from Barnes & Noble, which I figured would get him a couple of kids' paperback books. His first response — in fact his only response, which he made more than once — was that his mother had spent thirty dollars on me but I had spent only fifteen dollars on him. Jamal was skeptical of people's motives, a quality that I'm guessing has served him well but one that did not inspire warm feelings. Once, I bought him a journal, explaining that he might write in it when he had thoughts or feelings he didn't know what to do with. (Even Jamal's third-grade teacher thought that idea was a nonstarter.) When I gave him the journal, he said drily, "Woke up this morning, saw a bird out the window…"

Since reading and writing with Jamal was not doing much for either of us, and since it appeared that I was really in his life for other reasons, I decided I would take him to a few places. That resulted in the warmest moment we had together. One weekend in the spring of 2002, when a circus came to Brooklyn, he and I went. At some point during the goings-on, when everyone in the audience was standing for some reason, an announcer gave a shout-out to fathers and their children. I looked down at Jamal, and he looked up at me, and I put my arm around his shoulders, and we both smiled.

The decision to take him places also effectively ended our relationship. One Sunday I took him and The Pie to the movies. Jamal wanted to see one particular movie, whose title I have long since forgotten, but for some reason — the show times or the locations were inconvenient, or the movie seemed to me inappropriate, or something — we went instead to see a Japanese animated film. Jamal was silent and obviously pissed off going into the movie, he was silent and obviously pissed off afterward, and in the theater he leaned sideways with his head resting on his palm, refusing to dignify with words the grievous wrong I was doing him. After the movie I dropped The Pie at our apartment and then took Jamal home. The silent tension between us for those fifteen or twenty minutes, as we walked for block after block in the sunshine, was like a third presence. Outside his building, as he was about to go in, I leaned toward him and said angrily what I wanted him to know: something to the effect that you don't always get exactly what you want in this life, that if you can't at least appreciate what people try to do for you, soon they won't want to do anything. His response was exactly what I knew it would be. Without a word, he went inside the building.

Not long after that, I sent Darlene a note or an email saying that while I didn't feel like the reading was going anywhere, I wanted to continue doing things with Jamal. I like to think I meant it; I definitely *thought* I meant it — I was not, at least not consciously, looking for a way to ease out of my relationship with a kid whom I liked less and less and who certainly seemed to have no use for me. Soon afterward I ran into Darlene on the street. She was friendly. It was "a pity" about the reading, she said, but I could certainly continue to get together with Jamal. His weekends were now taken up with organized soccer, but when the season was over, we could resume our outings. I said that would be great.

Yeah. Let's have lunch sometime. The soccer season had passed, and so had the one after that, when I ran into Darlene again. I asked how Jamal was doing. She shrugged, with an expression that meant, *What is there to say*. I have not seen her or Jamal since.

There would be no point in talking about the guilt I felt, and continue to feel, over the way things went with Jamal. The larger point—and the reason I have shared this story—is that our good intentions do not always translate into effective action, when they translate into action at all. To do even that, they must first get past the villain of this book, that inescapable fact—that dragon—of the human condition: indifference.

Indifference is not always as cold a concept as it sounds, which is part of its deviousness. It does not have to be the stone-faced absence of caring; sometimes it takes the form of the hollowness at the core of our noblest intentions.

I am a movie buff (and sometime film critic), and one movie illustrates what I mean: John Sayles's wonderful *The Brother from Another Planet* (1984), starring the black actor Joe Morton as a mute extraterrestrial on the run from intergalactic slave catchers (played by Sayles and David Strathairn). The Brother crash-lands in Harlem, where he is taken for just another homeless New Yorker; someone leads him to the office of a black social worker, played by the underrated Tom Wright. The sequence I am thinking of is brief, wordless, and profound. The Wright character arrives at work to find the Brother sitting in front of his desk. Overworked, no doubt underpaid, tired, not thrilled to see the apparently homeless Brother, the social worker sighs — and then sticks his hand out, so the Brother can slap him five. This gesture says, *I'm not perfect. But I'll do what I can for you. We're in this together.*

In that scene, Tom Wright plays the man whom a part of me wants to be: someone whose whole life is helping others without thought of reward or recognition, a person who doesn't even realize how selfless he is. (Jeannette Bocanegra is one of his real-life counterparts. Another is my sister Wanda, a clergywoman, mental health professional, and activist.) But I am not that man — no writer is — and I never will be. Since Jamal, my efforts to effect change have consisted mainly of attending marches and rallies, calling the offices of members of Congress about this or that issue, and volunteering during election seasons — working the phone banks, registering voters on the street, knocking on doors. This past January, on a long list of things I wanted to do this year, I wrote, "Volunteer more." As I write this, the year is half over, and I have not stepped up my volunteering. Like most of us, I am very busy, but that is not the whole story.

Still: even if I am not the Tom Wright character, I can do better. It is, I think, a matter of overcoming indifference in the only way that works: seeing what's in it for me. Maybe this applies, as well, to the indifference of the white guy who doesn't consider himself a racist but voted for Trump and doesn't see why people of color should hate him for that. Maybe if he were made to understand that if conditions were better in the neighborhood where his precious children might accidentally find themselves one day, their experience there might be better, too. . .

* * *

As for the rest, it can be summed up by a true story I got secondhand, on Facebook, and by the reason I got it.

Two white men were stopped at a gas station. They talked about how great it was that Trump was president, and they laughed over the way liberals are so angry that "their guy" — Obama — is gone. Then one man told the other a joke. "What do they do with niggers in Canada? Melt 'em down to make hockey pucks!"

The story was recounted by the person who overheard it, who seemed — maybe because this was fresher news to him — even more disgusted than I was. His disgust was the reason he shared the story. He is a white man.

But of course there is more. Of the Big Three aside from plain, straight-up racism — indifference, ignorance, and denial — it is indifference that raises the hardest questions. Ignorance can be eroded, to an extent, with great pains taken on both sides; even denial, which suggests feelings of guilt, which in turn suggests the presence of a conscience, indicates the possibility — however dim — of a process of being uprooted, in this case from identification with either whiteness or the belief in America's perfection, and seeing more clearly afterward.

Indifference, however, is at the cold heart of the trouble, this American racial trouble of ours; and the question becomes whether this widespread indifference of so many people to the fates of so many others is seen as antithetical to, or intrinsically bound up with, America and one's identification as an American.

We have cited the view that the flip side of freedom is risk. Can a thing have two flip sides? If so, perhaps the other quality found on the cold, slimy, muddy, worm-ridden underside of the big flat rock of freedom, lying there alongside risk, is indifference — the absence of the obligation to give a damn about anybody else, king or beggar. All we are required to do, when we can manage even that, is to leave one another alone, which sounds fine, until it allows for an unqualified disaster like the election of Donald Trump.

If the flip side has a flip side, it is that freedom, to the extent that black Americans have it — being left to our own devices, in ways sometimes good, sometimes bad, and not having to adhere to a central culture, whether that culture is Chinese or Icelandic — leaves space for a culture of our own. Without black people's experience in America, there would be no blues, no jazz, no Billie Holiday or Otis Redding or Nina Simone, no Baldwin or Murray, none of the wonderful riffs on the English language that is black slang (and often becomes white slang), none of what makes us *us*.

To follow that argument to its logical conclusion,

of course, is to argue for the benefits of slavery. You see what we're up against. It is as if we owe our existence to rape. In fact, that is exactly the case.

This may be an unsolvable puzzle, a question with no answer. Here is an easier one: What attitude does one take toward descendants of those who committed that very crime against one's ancestors — and who did it without thinking of its silver lining? For me, much depends on the attitude of the individual descendant. *Just remember they're not all the same, just like we're not all the same.*

* * *

It is not uncommon for a person, especially a black person, to talk about injustices and to be asked in response, "What are you complaining about? You're doing fine" — as if having a happy life disqualifies one from acknowledging the pain of others.

Those responders are right about one thing, though, at least in my case: the part about doing fine. I have had a good life, in large part for the usual reasons. I have been married for a quarter-century to a woman I love. I have two great children. I have had the good fortune to find one or two things I can do reasonably well, well enough to get immense pleasure out of pursuing them. And then there is this:

The joy of what I call being "plugged in." I don't use the term the way others do; I don't mean anything having to do with networking or using electronic devices. I refer, instead, to the excitement I feel over the prospect of learning ever more about the art forms I love. Something akin to faith is involved in the continued desire to learn, a faith that there is value in it, that it is all *for* something, even if the things learned prove to be their own value. I keep reading, keep looking at art, keep watching films, keep listening to jazz. Jazz involves a tireless exploration that nonetheless acknowledges the limitlessness of what can be explored. One day recently I walked over the Brooklyn Bridge while listening, on my headphones, to "Alfie's Theme," by Sonny Rollins, an experience I recommend to everyone; Rollins's wonderful, extended tenor sax solo seems to *search*, to bore a hole through the earth in its investigation of ideas, even as it suggests the possibility of more to investigate, and the still greater possibility, nay, the certainty, that we will never know it all.

It is a source of both anguish and comfort, though mostly comfort, that I will never get to the bottom of any of it, that I will simply explore as much as I can. And yet, every so often, comes a voice whispering: *For what?* Having almost certainly passed the halfway point of my life, what is it that I am so studiously working toward — a body of knowledge and insight that will one day reach its glorious peak, so that I can then…die?

The answer to this is no less true for being a cliché: it's the journey, not the destination, etc., yes. The beauty of this chestnut is that it can apply to other areas of life.

The drawback is that it is easier to think than to feel. To the question, *What is the point of raising a family when your children simply grow up and leave?* I can answer: at least part of the point is the memories of raising them, the memories they share from the journey, too; except that those memories make me miss them more, not less. The question about the point can be asked about marriage, too. I sometimes feel as if I am in silent communion with my wife's parents, who died when she was so young, whom I never met and who never knew of my existence — as if they have entrusted her care to me, not because she can't take care of herself, but because we, all of us, need caring for, protecting; and yet there is no protection, not in the end. Sometimes when my wife and I hug each other, tightly, I feel as if we are trying to hold off the inevitable.

None of this is to say that the "journey" concept is not useful. Its value, I think, lies partly in its appreciation of the beauty of the parts as opposed to a concern for the validity of the whole. I may not see my children every day, but I can still smile when I think, for example, of one particular evening. Amy and I and our girls, then ten and six, stretched out on our beds at the Windswept Motel in Point Pleasant, New Jersey; as we watched the 2004 Olympic Games on television, after a day of hanging out at the beach and the pool, I thought to myself that I would take nothing in the world in exchange for where I was.

And this appreciation of the part, the individual, as opposed to the whole, can apply as well to groups of people.

* * *

Don't worry about what people think of you. You worry about what you think of yourself and that will take care of everything else. If Trump's election makes me change who I am, then who was I, really?

* * *

To pass the halfway point of one's life is, of course, to see the earlier points with new eyes. I was twenty-four years old when James Baldwin died, in 1987, at sixty-three. By being in the right place at the right time — in other words, through sheer dumb luck — I attended Baldwin's funeral. Oh, the pomp, the majesty, the number of illustrious writers who were in attendance; it was almost enough to make one forget what I mainly think of when I recall it now: the end of a human life, of its possibilities, of hope for what that next book might accomplish, of what might still be rectified. "This is a very sad occasion," the book editor who was then my boss said to me. He was reminding us both, I think.

When one is twenty-four, the thought of death at sixty-three may not rate more than a shrug; when sixty-three is visible on the horizon, things look a bit different. But of course death, which on the one hand gives life meaning — as rules give meaning to a game — is on the other hand *always* and immeasurably sad, sad for all of us (as John Donne knew), pointing out the pathetic nature of human limitation, turning us all finally into children, wide-eyed, blinking, helpless against what we cannot understand.

I think of Albert Murray. I was not present when he died, though I feel like I was. I saw him for the last time in his Harlem apartment in June 2013, when I was fifty and he was ninety-seven. He was lying in the bed that had been set up in the living room. His daughter, Michele, getting on in years herself by then, was with us. I don't think that Murray, my friend of nearly two decades, knew who I was, at least not in the way we think of such knowledge. He had become hard of hearing, and communicating with him was difficult. One thing had not changed: he was still a talker. The difference was that I could not understand most of what he said. But he was saying it passionately — his eyes were wide open, eyebrows raised, as if in wonder at the ideas with which he was grappling, whatever they were. Eventually I sensed that it was time for me to leave. "Give him a kiss," Michele said to me, and I kissed my old friend's forehead, and then I left, and later that summer, Murray left, too.

And of course death is not the only human limitation. As a young, precociously skilled writer, Joan Didion penned a number of essays whose collective subtext was a lament over the change that was as inevitable as it was sad, and as one loses friends, and sees family members drift away, one may join in her lament. Some things do not change, though, even as we age, even as generations come and go, and one thing that does not change is the human need to believe in something, to feel rooted. Didion herself demonstrated this other form of human limitation; even as curious, searching, and clear-sighted an intellect as hers needed to be grounded by ideas, and when she found she lacked those ideas ("the production was never meant to be improvised"), she suffered.

Another word for this necessary acquiescence to human limitation is faith. There is something appealing and romantic about the plight of the priest who has knocked up against this limitation, who has lost his faith — unless, of course, the priest happens to be you. Faith is sometimes sorely tested by conditions on the ground. But faith, by its very definition, is the absence of proof. Sometimes it can mean continuing on what feels like the wrong path, in the hope that it will intersect with the right one; sometimes it is like humming and bluffing your way through the part of the song you don't know until you get to the part you can sing. *Fake it 'til you make it.* Perhaps my equivalent of Christian faith is my belief in treating everyone as an individual and my belief in the positive, unbreakable link between black people and America. Sometimes these ideas feel like the core of my being; at other times they seem to defy reason.

But maybe even I get to be unreasonable sometimes. Unreasonableness, actually, has played a part in my life, making appearances at rare but key moments. Being unreasonable gave me a writing career, leading me to keep plugging away after a reasonable person would have quit. And then there is this: when I was born, my mother and father already had three children, ten and older, my mother was thirty-eight — at the time a scandalous age to have a child — and there was not a lot of money. I was not an "Oops" baby, though; despite everything, my mother wanted to experience motherhood, from the beginning, just once more, and I owe everything I am, and have, and ever will have, to her unreasonable desire.

And there is a practical side to all this unreasonable reasonableness. Black people need allies. How long would you remain an ally if you were white and kept hearing *White people ain't shit?*

Another thought: Donald Trump is not America. He is merely — so far, knock wood — its worst-ever representative on the world stage. His is the absence of a presidency; he is that nightmare substitute teacher from your childhood writ large, favoring the mean kids — who just act meaner — and caring nothing about what happens as long as we all say the Pledge of Allegiance. He is the substitute-in-chief, presiding over what one must hope is the temporary ruin of Classroom USA.

And still another thought: perhaps as important as judging people as individuals is *being* an individual. I have tried to point out both the inevitability and the dangers of a sense of rootedness; but perhaps an antidote to the dangers is a strong sense of individuality. A balance of rootedness and individuality makes one a kind of tree, firmly attached to the world, sharing its fate, yet standing separate and as free as one can ever be, reaching high, up where everything can be seen.

So much to see. Like Philip Smith, founder of the National African American Gun Association, I will go to Africa one day. In the meantime, after returning to New York from Atlanta, curious about the experience of going to a gun range, I thought I would find one.

I should explain. Like many, I feel impotent rage any time there is a mass shooting followed by talk of "thoughts and prayers" from politicians whose strings — attached at the other end to NRA puppeteers — you can almost see. I consider the gun crisis — and it is a crisis — a stain on our country.

So, no, I am not a right-wing Second Amendment nut. What I am, deep inside, is a little boy, one who was raised on cop shows. Like every American male my age, I am guessing, I harbor a fantasy about carrying a badge and a gun. And so, introduced to the idea of firing a weapon in a controlled environment, acting out just a tiny bit of my fantasy, I thought: Why not?

The range I found was Westside Rifle & Pistol Range, on West 20th Street in Manhattan. It is in an office building, below ground, accessible by stairs. Going down, I heard loud shots, which got my heart racing a little, more in fear than excitement. In the offices there were two TVs on: one, in an empty seating area, played a soap opera, featuring the worst actors I have ever seen in my life; the other, near a rectangular table, played an old Western movie with plenty of shooting. Several customers, mostly men, more than one wearing fatigue pants, sat around the table, waiting to shoot and swapping gun stories. Signs on the wall read "Making good people helpless will not make bad people harmless" and "My right to own a gun protects your right to tell me I can't." Jesus, what was I doing here? Well, I was here now.

Eventually an instructor led me and three other people to a back room to show us how to use .22 rifles. After that, we each manually loaded ten magazines with five bullets apiece, put on glasses or protective eye gear, and headed to the range. I was, at first, careful to the point of near-paralysis to make sure the safety was on until it was time to fire. Then I began to relax. I was a better shot than I had thought. I had wondered what would come to mind as I prepared to fire: Gregory Peck as Atticus Finch, shouldering the rifle to shoot a rabid dog in *To Kill a Mockingbird*? The crazed man shooting the time traveler Billy Pilgrim in Kurt Vonnegut's *Slaughterhouse-Five*? But there was no such literary high-mindedness. Mostly, I had fun.

As I stood amid the smell of smoke and the *plink* of gold-colored shell casings hitting the floor, a kind of window opened in my mind, a peek into another life. What if I were a different sort of person, who had traveled a different path? What if I were a black man whose upbringing had been rougher, who was harder, who had been shown less compassion, who had been encouraged not to *think* quite so much but to *do*? What if, seeing the wrong done to dark-skinned people, I didn't worry about the why but only the what? I might embrace simple logic, simple feeling—I might have no trouble deciding who the enemy was. I might find others like me, others who saw things happening in their country they didn't think could happen anymore, others who thought one bad turn deserved another, others who finally began to wonder, like me, why we were killing each other when the real enemy was elsewhere. Guns would be a regular part of my life, this rougher, simpler life, not just in the shooting range but in my home, on my night table, a dark weapon with its satisfying weight tucked into my baggy jean shorts, making a small bulge under my loose-fitting T-shirt, as I walked the streets, maybe your street, alert to signs of disrespect.

And as I peeked into that life, I realized how easy it had become, here in the safe and controlled environment of the gun range, how very, very easy it had become to pull the trigger.

Acknowledgments

Infinite thanks go out to the crew at Other Press — including Alexandra Poreda, Iisha Stevens, Yvonne Cárdenas, Janice Goldklang, Jessica Greer, and especially the publisher, Judith Gurewich, for her vision, her obstinacy, her ability to make me see my own obstinacy, and her success in overcoming it. A great many thanks to my friend and agent extraordinaire, Timothy Hays. And much much gratitude to the following people: Ken Josing; Mike Davison; Jeannette Bocanegra; Philip Smith; Dick Wilbur; Mishi Faruqee; Donna May; Susan Kaufman; Adam Shatz; Eric Banks and Melanie Rehak of the New York Institute for the Humanities; Chris Carduff; Tom Rayfiel; Charles Hawley; and my wife, Amy Peck.

Clifford Thompson's work has appeared in publications including *The Best American Essays 2018*, *Washington Post*, *Wall Street Journal*, *Threepenny Review*, and *Village Voice*. He is the recipient of a Whiting Award for nonfiction and teaches at New York University, Sarah Lawrence College, and the Bennington Writing Seminars. He lives in Brooklyn, New York.